# Unity and Language

## UNC | COLLEGE OF ARTS AND SCIENCES
Germanic and Slavic Languages and Literatures

From 1949 to 2004, UNC Press and the UNC Department of Germanic & Slavic Languages and Literatures published the UNC Studies in the Germanic Languages and Literatures series. Monographs, anthologies, and critical editions in the series covered an array of topics including medieval and modern literature, theater, linguistics, philology, onomastics, and the history of ideas. Through the generous support of the National Endowment for the Humanities and the Andrew W. Mellon Foundation, books in the series have been reissued in new paperback and open access digital editions. For a complete list of books visit www.uncpress.org.

# Unity and Language

A Study in the Philosophy of Johann Georg Hamann

JAMES C. O'FLAHERTY

UNC Studies in the Germanic Languages and Literatures
Number 6

Copyright © 1952

This work is licensed under a Creative Commons CC BY-NC-ND license. To view a copy of the license, visit http://creativecommons.org/licenses.

Suggested citation: O'Flaherty, James. *Unity and Language: A Study in the Philosophy of Johann Georg Hamann*. Chapel Hill: University of North Carolina Press, 1952. DOI: https://doi.org/10.5149/9781469658124_OFlaherty

Library of Congress Cataloging-in-Publication Data
Names: O'Flaherty, James C.
Title: Unity and language : A study in the philosophy of Johann Georg Hamann / by James C. O'Flaherty.
Other titles: University of North Carolina Studies in the Germanic Languages and Literatures ; no. 6.
Description: Chapel Hill : University of North Carolina Press, [1952] Series: University of North Carolina Studies in the Germanic Languages and Literatures. | Includes bibliographical references.
Identifiers: LCCN 52004007 | ISBN 978-1-4696-5811-7 (pbk: alk. paper) | ISBN 978-1-4696-5812-4 (ebook)
Subjects: Hamann, Johann Georg, 1730-1788.
Classification: LCC PD25 .N6 NO. 6 | DCC 193/ .9

To
LUCY AND JAMES DANIEL

## ACKNOWLEDGMENTS

This study is a revision of my doctoral dissertation, "The Linguistic Foundations of Hamann's Concept of Unity," written in 1950 at the University of Chicago under Professor Wilhelm Pauck. I shall ever feel profoundly obligated to Professor Pauck for the inspiration of his lectures and his excellent counsel, to Professors James Luther Adams and John G. Kunstmann for their constructive criticism and encouragement during the writing of the dissertation, to Dr. Walter Lowrie, who encouraged me to publish the dissertation, and finally to Dr. Richard Jente for his wise editorial assistance.

I wish to record here my gratitude to my wife, Lucy Ribble O'Flaherty, for her patience above and beyond the call of duty during the writing of the dissertation and likewise for her editorial assistance. Further, I wish to thank Dr. G. G. Grubb for his assistance in reading the proof.

I desire also to express my deep appreciation to Wake Forest College for the financial grant which helped make publication possible.

J. C. O'F.

# TABLE OF CONTENTS

**INTRODUCTION** ................................................................................................. 1
Contemporary concern with rôle of language in cognition, 1. Basal importance of unity-concept in Hamann's philosophy, 2-3. Foundations of unity-concept sought in language, 3-4. Hamann's aversion to system, 4-5. Hamann no metaphysical monist, 5. Opposition to Enlightenment, 6-7. Nadler's current research and publications, 7-8. Qualified optimism regarding Hamann's significance, 8. Author's procedure in translating, 8-9.

**CHAPTER I. THE PRIMACY OF NATURAL LANGUAGE** ................... 10
Unger's perpetuation of the Hegelian view of Hamann, 10-11. Revelation and natural language, 11-12. Imagery of the Old Testament, 13. Self-knowledge, 13-14. Nature, 14-15. Nature and the parabolic expression of truth, 15-16. Definitions of the terms "natural," "poetic," and "abstract language," 16-17. Antithesis of natural and abstract language, 17. Hamann's emphasis upon linguistic form, 17-20. Language reform as rational control of natural language, 20-23. Hamann's interest in linguistics, 23-26. Natural language as a clue to the nature of reality, 26-32.

**CHAPTER II. LANGUAGE AND EXPERIENCE** .................................... 33
Verbalistic nature of all cognitive experience, 33. Appeal to *principia coincidentiae oppositorum* as a linguistic principle, 33-34. Relation of thought and language in the philosophy of representative thinkers, 34-35. Reason and experience cognitively effective only in language, 35-39. Uniting bond of thought and language mysterious, 39. Verbalistic interpretation of experience opposed to mutual identification of self, nature, and God, 39-42. Socratic ignorance as an appeal to experience, 42-44. Genius as the creator of new symbolic syntheses, 45. Human living as symbolic action, 46.

**CHAPTER III. THE DUALITY IN UNITY OF LANGUAGE** ................. 47
Failure of interpreters to analyse Hamann's idea of linguistic unity, 47. Identification of abstractions as relational symbolism, 48-51. Fundamental relations of time and space experientially derived, 52-54. Revelation within framework of time and space, 54-55. Limitations of subject-object dualism in interpretation of Hamann's thought, 55-56. Hamann's general relativism, 56-60. Reality of objects, 60. Epistemological status of faith, 60-61. Relational symbols of ordinary language as archetypes of abstractions, 61-63. Unger's misunderstanding of Hamann's idea of linguistic unity, 63-65. Religious implications of unity of language, 65-66. Concept

viii                    UNITY AND LANGUAGE

of linguistic unity as key to understanding of Hamann, 66-67.
Linguistic philosophy in eighteenth century, 67-68. "Sense-unit,"
68. Categories of language and universal grammar, 68-69. Categories of language and Goethe's *Urphänomen*, 69-70. Hamann's
criticism of Herder's theory of origin of language, 70-72. Divine
origin of language, 72. Recapitulation, 72-73.

CHAPTER IV.  REASON AND EXPERIENCE ............................................. 74
Linguistic unity destroyed by excessive ratiocination, 74. Critique
of abstractions as subjective symbolism, 75-77. Lessing's theory of
revelation seen as a rejection of revelational experience, 77-79.
Restoration of analytic judgment implied in Lessing's theory, 79-
80. Discontinuity between reason and history in Lessing's thought,
80. Contemporary revaluation of Hamann's critique of Kantianism,
81-83. Similarities and differences between Hamann and Kant,
83-84. Linguistic criterion applied to Kant, 85. Hamann's *Metacritique of the Purism of Pure Reason*, 85-87. Reinterpretation of
Hamann's critique of Kantianism, 87-89. Hamann's anticipation
of twentieth century criticism of Kant, 89-90. Ground of linguistic
unity exterior to mind, 90-91. Philosophy of "verbalism" opposed
to Enlightenment, 91-92. Theological implications of bipolar nature
of language, 92-93. Hamann's tendency to draw inferences from
natural language to reality, 94.

CHAPTER V.  SUMMARY AND CONCLUSION
Hamann's linguistic philosophy not a basis for metaphysical
monism 95-96. Faith as basis of Hamann's philosophy of unity,
96-97. Dualistic implications of Hamann's epistemology, 97-98.
Aversion to abstraction and the scientific spirit, 98-99. Hamann's
inconsistency in opposing abstraction, 99. Hamann's vacillating
confidence in language theory, 99. Permanent importance of
critique of abstractions and covert doctrine of relations in interpretation of Hamann, 99-100.

VI.   NOTES ........................................................................................ 101-113

VII.  BIBLIOGRAPHY ............................................................................ 114-118

VIII. INDEX OF PERSONS ..................................................................... 119-121

# INTRODUCTORY NOTE

Professor O'Flaherty, descended, as his name attests, from a loyal Irish race, became by a trick of fortune a Protestant, whereas I, descended from Scottish Covenanters, have become a Catholic of sorts. In spite of our excentric trajectories, we were brought into conjunction by our interest in Hamann, and are united all the more closely because, so far as we can tell, few other Americans have shown an interest in this great man. But we have reason to hope that such celebrity as accrues to us by reason of our singular interest will not be lasting, for Hamann will not always be forgotten. Now, a century and a half after his death, Professor Nadler of the University of Vienna has just published a new biography which interprets Hamann as "The Witness of the *Corpus Mysticum*," and has commenced to publish in five volumes the most complete edition of his works and letters. It is vain to contend, like Michael and the devil, about the body of Hamann; for this good Protestant was buried as a good Catholic in the garden of Princess Gallitzin, where in the company of her pious court he had enjoyed "a foretaste of heaven", and upon his tomb was appropriately written simply "A Christian man."

Professor O'Flaherty insists that my pamphlet, "Johann Georg Hamann," published in 1950 by the Princeton Theological Seminary, is worth more than his Dissertation; but with the *pervervidum ingenium Scottorum* (to use Tacitus' characterization of my race which is easily roused to anger) I protest that it is far easier to write, as I have done, a sketch of this strange man's life than to illuminate, as he has done, the thought of the most enigmatic writer since Lao-tze and Herakleitos.

I was attracted to Hamann by Kierkegaard's admiration for him, which was expressed in the *Journal* by the exclamation, "Emperor!" on the occasion of his first encounter with this great man—as Napoleon had instructed his lackies to shout when they threw open before him the double doors, *de par in par,* as the Spanish say. Later I was struck by the admiration Goethe expressed for the Magus of the North, his polar opposite in matters of faith. And because of the candor and generosity he showed in this instance I form a loftier estimate of Goethe than ever before. "Deep calleth unto deep"—*Sag' welch ist tiefer!* exclaimed Rückert.

Walter Lowrie

Princeton, New Jersey.
September 12, 1951.

INTRODUCTION

When the intellectual history of the first half of the twentieth century is written, scholars will most certainly call attention to the extraordinary attempt in this period— and that in the most diverse quarters—to understand the peculiar rôle which language plays in the cognitive process. In order to note this emphasis one need but call to mind developments in several areas, e.g., the contemporary concern of the physicist with the validity of his mathematico-physical symbolism for the interpretation of reality; the flourishing growth of positivistic semantics; the current Soviet linguistic controversy (in which even Joseph Stalin appears in the guise of linguistic philosopher!); and finally the focussing of theological attention upon the *word* apparent on the one hand in the development of form-criticism and on the other hand in the emergence of the dialectical theology. Whether this general concern with various types of linguistic symbolism bespeaks an intellectual climate more fruitful than that which produced the medieval schoolman's debates about universals and particulars remains to be seen. But the emergence of this phenomenon in the first half of the twentieth century is a fact beyond dispute.

In such a period as this it is not at all strange that interest in Johann Georg Hamann should revive. For Hamann is preëminently the philosopher of language. Whatever divergent ramifications his thought may have—and they are many—the source of all that is most positive in his thinking is to be found in his philosophy of language. Hamann is not easy to interpret. Indeed, those who are even slightly familiar with his writings may feel that to put it this way is to make a classic understatement. But much that Hamann has to say can be understood, and this is sufficiently important to warrant attention. For better or worse, the day when Hamann, the so-called "Magus of the North," could be contemptuously dismissed as an obscurantist has passed. For a thinker who defied the philosophic conventions of his time, and faced squarely the problem of the relation of thought and language speaks in a more contemporary idiom than those of his compeers who ignored the problem or gave it but insignificant attention.

In this study no attempt has been made to establish Hamann as a present-day oracle. I have rather undertaken to discover the major outlines of his thought and to determine the extent to which it yields permanently valid insights. It will be seen that Hamann was in many ways a child of the eighteenth century. But it will also be seen, I believe, that what he has to say is of more abiding value than many critics have supposed.

The basal importance of Hamann's concept of unity for an understanding of his thought has long been recognized. Thus Goethe wrote nearly a century and a half ago in the twelfth book of his autobiography: "The main principle to which all Hamann's statements may be referred is the following: 'All that a man undertakes to perform, whether by deed or word or otherwise, must proceed from all his powers united; everything isolated is worthless'."[1] From one point of view this dictum may be accepted as an adequate statement of Hamann's main principle. Not only does he frequently state that he is interested in "nothing but the whole,"[2] but he repeatedly protests against the tendency of the rationalistic philosophers to destroy what he conceived to be the essential unity of existence. "The philosophers have always given truth a bill of divorcement," he wrote, "in that they have put asunder that which nature has joined together, and vice versa."[3] The complaint against the divisive tendency of reason is one of the most frequent refrains of the Hamannian writings, and indeed it underscores his demand for unity more effectively than his positive statements concerning the importance of the whole.

That the disagreement as to how Hamann's concept of unity should be understood is still very great, however, is attested by the fact that in recent years it has been interpreted on the one hand in terms of axiological theory[4] and on the other hand in terms of existential philosophy.[5] In spite of the acknowledged centrality of this concept in Hamann's philosophy, no systematic treatment of it has appeared up to the present time. This is particularly unfortunate, since a relegation of it to the background has the invariable result that, in one way or another, it obtrudes itself upon the discussion. Thus nothing is gained by the refusal to come to terms directly with this central idea.

The emphasis upon the importance of the concept of unity should not, however, be construed to mean that there is one principle which illuminates all areas of Hamann's thought. Such a claim would do violence to both the letter and spirit of his philosophy. Yet it may be asserted with confidence that, if one principle were to be singled out as most nearly definitive for his thought, it should have to be the principle of unity. Therefore, one cannot in the last resort quarrel with Goethe's formulation, though it may very well be doubted that he understood its full implication for Hamann.

It is, however, not my aim to treat Hamann's concept of unity from the psychological, metaphysical or purely theological standpoints. Indeed, this study is not so much concerned with a systematic treatment of the concept itself as with its foundations in Hamann's linguistic philosophy. To be sure, statements such as "my mind seems to comprehend nothing so well as the whole" (V,87) and "rather nothing than half" (G,V,405), suggest that the psychological factors in his demand for unity are very important, and Rudolf Unger finds them decisive.[6] On the other hand, such statements as "after all, the excision of each part depends upon the whole" (G,V,137) and "when a *single* truth reigns like the sun, that is *day*" (H.' italics. II,281), are invitations to a primarily metaphysical treatment of the unity-concept. For even though Hamann vigorously rejects the possibility of an "intuition of the one in the many" (VI,5), his philosophy of unity does have metaphysical implications, and Metzke has treated these implications as pointing to a new interpretation of reality.[7] Finally statements like "the *unity* of the Creator is reflected in the *dialect* of his works" (H.'s italics. II,276) and "to dissect a body and an event into its first elements means to desire to detect God's invisible being, his eternal power and Godhead" (II,17), are an invitation to a purely theological treatment of his idea of unity. Despite the potential fruitfulness of each of these approaches, I have adopted none of them, but have considered it far more imperative for an understanding of Hamann's philosophy to keep to the foundations of the unity-concept.

The frequency with which Hamann appeals to the unity of language as a basic principle strikes even his casual reader. This would suggest that the clearest possible understanding of his idea of linguistic unity is the indispensable propaedeutic to an interpretation of his total philosophy. Unger has dealt extensively with Hamann's language theory,[8] but, as we shall see in the sequel, his interpretation, despite its many merits, must finally be rejected. It shall be my concern to emphasize precisely those aspects of Hamann's linguistic philosophy which have either been ignored or misunderstood by Unger. This study, then, is chiefly concerned with language as the prismatic medium through which Hamann saw experience or reality. In order to accomplish my purpose, it will be necessary to appeal to his epistemological and theological principles, but these are subsidiary to the primary task of showing in what way Hamann conceived language to be a faithful surrogate for reality. Once his theory of language is grasped, an understanding of the rest of his thought inevitably follows. "With me," he wrote to Jacobi, in 1785, "it is neither a question of physics nor of theology, but of *language,* the mother of reason and revelation, their alpha and omega." (H.'s italics. G,V,122). Hamann once said of his philosophy, "It stands and walks with its feet on the ground, and can only reach heaven with its eyes, from a distance, from afar." (VII,400). In the following pages I shall undertake to show just how language constitutes this "ground" of his total philosophy. This does not mean that his thought may be reduced to a system, but it does mean that the consistency of large outline is recognized.

At this point a word should be said about Hamann's well-known aversion to system, for any coherent discussion of his thought presupposes some degree of consistency inhering in it, and therefore appears to be in opposition to his clearly announced principles. On numerous occasions he disclaims a desire for system on the ground that it is a hindrance to truth. "I am not equal to truths, principles, and systems" (I,497), he wrote to J. G. Lindner in 1759 in defense of his first important attack on the Enlightenment, the *Socratic Memoirs.* Some twenty-seven years later, he wrote to Jacobi, "System is in itself a hindrance to truth." (G,V,228). These and other utterances[9] similar in import simply constitute Hamann's own admission of a fact which is everywhere apparent to his readers. On the other hand, he does not completely abjure system, for in speaking of his writings, he says: "In all that chaos is a thread which the adept can find."[10] A clue to the manner in which he conceived it possible for system and chaos, order and disorder to exist side by side may be found in his characterization of the Bible: "In the Bible we find precisely the regular disorder which we discover in nature. All methods are to be regarded as go-carts of reason and as crutches of the same." (I,118). The student of Hamann must agree with Cassirer who maintains that Hamann's thought revolves about language, and that the degree of coherence residing in his thought is the result of its centripetal orientation to language.[11] The manner in which this occurs will become plain in the subsequent chapters of this study. The disorderly nature of Hamann's writings and his own disclaimer of system should not deter the commentator from the attempt to determine the degree of coherence which is actually present in his thought. The difficulty presented by the form of the Hamannian writings should serve, however, as a fair warning that concern with his ideas involves a very severe discipline. For Hamann both consciously and unconsciously puts his reader at grave disadvantage on almost every page of his writings. It is not without good reason that Unger describes Hamann as "the most obscure author of our modern literature."[12]

Since Hamann does not propound a basic idea as explanatory of the manifold of human existence, he cannot be called a monist in the sense in which this term may be predicated of Parmenides, Spinoza, Hegel or Bradley. His monism, if we are justified in applying that term to him at all, is a religious monism which finds in the "unity of the Creator" the ground and source of whatever unity may subsist in reality. We shall find that, according to Hamann, there is a unity given in human experience which is of basal importance for cognition; but since this unity is within experience it is simply a "parable" of the unity of ultimate reality, and a monistic system may not be predicated on the basis of it. Thus the only rationally demonstrable unity of prime importance for cognition is not the unity of the Creator but the unity of the *created*. Hegel's dictum that the "true is the whole" Hamann would doubtless accept, but not in the Hegelian sense. Hamann is no metaphysical monist. On his view, unaided reason cannot arrive at an adequate conception of the whole, for reason is essentially analytic and divisive in nature. Appealing to Paul's word concerning the atomistic nature of reason (I Corinthians, 13:12), Hamann says, "Our thoughts are nothing but fragments. Indeed, we know in part." (I,129).

Emphasizing as he did the unity of human existence, it is small wonder that Hamann set himself in array against what he conceived to be the divisive and fractional techniques of eighteenth-century rationalism both before and after the critical work of Kant. It was against the rationalist's sundering of the intimately interwoven and delicate fabric of human existence that Hamann strove. This accounts for his polemic and in many ways negative orientation to the chief intellectual currents of his time. Many critics have seen only the negative side of Hamann; for them he was simply a bizarre and splenetic Don Quixote, tilting against the windmills of the Enlightenment. For example, Hettner, who is one of the truly great historians of German literature, was misled into the following characterization of Hamann:

> Hamann's thought and feeling is almost exclusively negative. It is the Pietistic blustering against the freedom and independence of science, which has emerged from the authority of the Bible, and against its alleged presumption.[13]

There can be no doubt that the mature Hamann hated the rationalism of the Enlightenment with all the intensity of his deeply emotional nature. But in the last resort he, too, was the child of the Enlightenment in an important sense, and shared with its other adherents at least an endlessly questing spirit and an attitude of relentless criticism of authoritarian pretensions. If he saw in the rationalistic proponents of the Enlightenment the most dangerous pretenders to authority, he may be considered as the Enlightenment turning upon itself. Indeed, he aptly described his own work as a "metacriticism" (VII,1-16), i.e., a criticism of the contemporary critical philosophy.

Hamann's most effective blow against the Enlightenment, however, was something apart from the mighty flood of indictments and vituperative jeremiads which issued from his pen. It is to be found in his linguistically-grounded idea of unity, for it was that idea, clothed in its peculiar but powerful form, which made him as Jakob Minor says, "the father of the Storm and Stress Period"[14] of German literature. When the young Goethe listened to Herder in Strasbourg, and was converted from the rococo-versification of his Leipzig days, he was really hearing the voice of Herder's master, Hamann. Though Goethe never encountered Hamann personally, but only indirectly through

Herder's doctrines and through Hamann's writings, it was nevertheless the remote influence of the Magus which freed the young Goethe from slavish obedience to the prevailing literary rationalism, and enabled him to find in the unity of his own experience, in the natural togetherness of feeling and thought, the true sources of his own creativity.[15] If Hettner's judgment upon Hamann were correct, there would be no way of explaining the liberating, positive influence of Hamann upon Goethe and other adherents of the Storm and Stress in Germany.[16] Of particular interest today is Hamann's influence on Kierkegaard,[17] and here again we come upon another positive aspect of his work. Even a brief list of the greatest thinkers and writers who have found Hamann a primarily constructive influence is imposing: Herder, Goethe, Jean Paul, Kierkegaard, and, in our own day, Brunner. Despite the controversy which the name of Hamann has always evoked in Germany, there can be no doubt that he is one of the genuine immortals of German history. It is interesting to note that a sketch of Hamann's life is included in a modern dictionary of biography which is limited to accounts of the lives of German notables from Arminius to Erich Ludendorff.[18]

One of the most interesting and important developments in the history of Hamannian research is taking place at the present time. In fact, it must be said that this development is the most important from the standpoint of pure research. At this writing, the first two volumes of Hamann's complete works have just appeared in Vienna under the able editorship of Josef Nadler.[19] The remaining volumes of this work are scheduled to appear at intervals during 1952. For the first time in history, all of the Hamannian writings will be available in print.[20] This will be the consummation of the wish not only of Hamann himself, but also of Goethe.[21] What results this will have for scholarship in this area remains to be seen.[22] Moreover, Nadler has written a well documented and thoroughly readable biography of Hamann based on his long acquaintance with the unpublished manuscripts.[23] In recent days these volumes have come into my hands, but unfortunately they arrived too late to serve as source material. An examination of them, however, reveals that they offer no material which would substantially alter the argument of this study. In this latest development in our field, we find Hettner's opinion of Hamann again implicitly called in question, for we have before us at the present time the edifying spectacle of the turning of a leading German scholar to the Hamann-problem. This, in conjunction with the prospect of the appearance of Hamann's collected works in the near future, is sufficient cause for rejoicing on the part of those who have labored in this field.

Although I believe that the present investigation of Hamann's linguistic philosophy discloses some grounds for optimism with reference to its ultimate significance, any feeling of this kind must be tempered by a sober awareness of the severe limitations of the Hamannian thought and literary style.[24] For, as Hegel aptly remarks, Hamann is characterized by a "perfectly concentrated intensity," and attains to "no kind of expansion, whether of imagination or of thought."[25] Or, as Kierkegaard more vividly expresses it in his *Concluding Unscientific Postscript*: "With all his life and soul, to the last drop of blood, he is concentrated in a single word . . . . ."[26] Hamann's procedure required the compression of his thought into the briefest possible space and the search for more and more comprehensive symbols in the attempt to say everything at once. This is a source of both strength and weakness. At its best, it enables him to epitomize in remarkable language his greatest insights. At its worst, it is productive of hard kernels of hopelessly obscure allusions. There is, nevertheless, much in Hamann's writings which is quite lucid, and his frequent obscurity should simply be accepted as one of the permanent conditions of research in this area. Because of developments within the field of linguistic philosophy in the last half century,[27] modern scholarship should be in a better position than that of an earlier day to do justice to his more luminous insights into the nature of language. If this is true, Hamann's foretaste of the "abilities of a better posterity" (II,114) may not in the last resort prove to have been illusory.

A final introductory word should be said about my procedure in translating passages from Hamann. As may be readily surmised, Hamann is a very difficult writer to translate. For, in his conception, style is an individual and private matter. "Our individuality," he wrote in this connection, "must become effective in every phrase and in every period."[28] To this principle he adhered as faithfully as the nature of language permits. With reference to this subject, Hegel wrote, "Hamann's writings do not so much have style as that they are style through and through."[29] By this he apparently meant that Hamann did not superficially adopt the conventionalities of language, but struggled to inform his expressions with the spirit peculiar to him. It is certainly true that one must read his own words to sense the full power of his mastery of language. In this study, in which we are chiefly concerned with his ideas and not with his literary creativity, the ineluctable loss of aesthetic power in translation will not be felt too much. Inasmuch as translations are one means whereby the considerable barrier which separates Hamann from the English-speaking public may be partially overcome, I have translated all citations occuring in the text, but not those occuring in the notes.[30]

## CHAPTER I

## THE PRIMACY OF NATURAL LANGUAGE

Hamann's language theory has always been a source of great attraction and disappointment at the same time. For his insights which seem momentarily to throw a flash of light upon the residual problems of language and knowledge appear quite inconsistent and exasperatingly obscurantist, when they are gathered together and considered in relation to one another. Rudolf Unger, beyond all doubt the most energetic and thorough Hamannian scholar before Nadler, attempts in *Hamann's Language Theory in Relation to His Philosophy* to explicate the theory in a coherent if not systematic fashion. Fascinated as he obviously is with the challenge of his subject, he makes it quite clear that he expects nothing from it as a theory of language capable of standing on its own feet.[1] The language theory is the one positive side of Hamann's work which has had no historically visible effect in the sense in which the language theories of Herder and Humboldt have. Its only value, he further contends, lies in the fact that it serves to illuminate the historical personality and achievement of its author.[2] These conclusions, stemming as they do from one whose concern with Hamann has been long and intelligent, are indeed depressing to those who should expect more of Hamann. They are even more so, when one realizes that both Hamann and his commentators are in substantial agreement as to the centrality of the language theory in all the manifold facets of his thought.[3]

Because of the great influence which Unger has exerted, and continues to exert, upon the interpretation of Hamann, and because of my own deviation from his version of the language theory—a disagreement which will become plain in a subsequent chapter—it will be well to turn aside momentarily from the primary task in order to examine Unger's assumptions. There can be no question that Unger accepts the viewpoint of Hegel with regard to Hamann. That viewpoint is as follows: Hamann's writings are noteworthy as a reflection of the "inconceivable singularity of their author." They constitute, however, "an exhausting riddle," and in order to understand them, one must look beyond them, presumably to the sources of his thought.[4] It is clear from Unger's method, which involves an amazingly thorough research into Hamann's intellectual environment (but unfortunately not so thorough with regard to the political, economic, and social environment), from his conclusions, and from specific remarks concerning Hegel's interpretation[5] that he has on the whole adopted the Hegelian view of Hamann.

One can understand the willingness to acquiesce in the judgment of so great a thinker as Hegel; yet such a view virtually denies to Hamann's ideas any validity in themselves. Unger's only explanation of Hamann's continued influence is to point to the singular personality of the Magus as expressed in his writings. It is indeed difficult to see how it could be Hamann's personality or individuality alone which makes his reckoning with the great minds of his own day a matter of interest to contemporary philosophers. For example, Metzke, who disagrees with Unger's basic orientation to Hamann, strives for a deeper understanding of the latter precisely as a philosopher, holding that the man who gave Herder's philosophy the decisive impulse, who carried on prolonged philosophical discussions with Jacobi, and who took up the battle over central philosophical issues with Hume, Mendelssohn, and Kant should greatly concern the historian of philosophy.[6] It is further difficult to see how Hamann's influence could be widely felt in succeeding generations in the areas of *belles lettres,* philosophy, and religion (during World War II letters dealing with Hamann's theology were sent regularly to theologically inclined German prisoners of war[7]), if we have here to do exclusively with a remarkable individual. Certainly Goethe's prophecy that Hamann would someday become for the German people a "codex" similar to Vico for the Italian people[8] is meaningless, if one sees his ideas as of secondary importance only. At any rate, I am committed to the view that, while it must be conceded that Hamann was no systematic thinker and that his personality was truly remarkable, the attempt to do justice to his ideas should, nevertheless, be seriously undertaken.

Having seen that there is reason to question Unger's interpretation of Hamann's significance in general, we may now turn to a study of the language theory without the prepossession that might otherwise unduly influence our conclusions.

It is a fundamental doctrine of Hamann's linguistic philosophy that ordinary human language is, to use Bergson's phrase, "molded on reality." This conviction was largely a by-product of his conversion experience in London in 1758. For it was through the instrumentality of the Bible, the written word, which he experienced as at once divine and human, that he was converted. But this written word necessitated the condescension of God to speak in the natural idiom of the people concerning what appears to human reason as "little contemptible events" (I,219) and "humanly foolish, indeed sinful actions." (I,87). The divine revelation was not tailored to fit the requirements of the rationalistic philosophers, who would have demanded a more intellectual formulation. (I,57-58;cf.61,223). That God had chosen to speak the ordinary language of the people concerning humble events rather than the technical language of the philosophers concerning abstruse matters never ceased to impress Hamann. Here we find the root of that abiding interest and confidence in natural language which is so characteristic of his thought until the end. Here, too, we find the root of his abiding suspicion of abstract language.

In choosing to speak the language of the people in poetic fashion,[9] God had ennobled that language, and had made it once and for all clear that knowledge about the meaning of life as a whole must always be cast in this form. It was not simply a form adopted for the masses who do not understand the language of the philosophers;[10] it is the only language in which God can speak even to the philosophers. For philosophers are also men with sensory natures, which they may despise but cannot circumvent.

> The Scriptures cannot speak with us as human beings otherwise than in parables, because all our knowledge is sensory, figurative, and because reason makes the images of external things everywhere into signs of more abstract, more intellectual concepts. (I, 99).

That is to say, the tendency of reason is always to reinterpret the "images of external things" or objects of everyday experience by means of the abstraction of certain characteristic features from them, and by the substitution of the abstract signs for the familiar signs of the vernacular. In this process two things happen: first, a part is substituted for the whole; secondly, the emotional associations or connotations are sloughed off. For

Hamann this process means not only a mutilation of language, but also a concomitant restriction of meaning to ultimately insignificant fragments of reality. "All mortal creatures," he says elsewhere, "are only able to see the truth and the essence of things in parables." (I,88).

In reply to Michaelis' strictures concerning the pictorial, figurative language of the Old Testament as unworthy of deity, Hamann wrote: "*Senses* and *emotions* speak and understand nothing but *images*. The entire treasury of human *knowledge* and *felicity* consists in *images*." (H.'s italics. II,259). The idea that all knowledge is "sensory, figurative" Hamann always espoused subsequent to his conversion. Here we are at the bed-rock of his linguistic philosophy, for apart from this idea one cannot begin to understand his thought. In the *Aesthetics in a Nutshell* (1762) he sums up his attitude toward the importance of the Scripture in understanding the primacy of natural language. The "extinct language of nature," which belonged to man in the childhood of the race, must now be consciously and deliberately regained by "crusades" and even by "old wives' cunning." (II,293).

It is evident from what has been said that Hamann's point of departure for an understanding of reality was his own existence and not the observable properties of objects scientifically conceived. "*Homo sum,*" he wrote, "the basis of all other relations" (VII,145), and "in the word *homo sum*" is "a world of ergo's according to my taste." (VI,286). Adopting for the moment the generally alien Leibnizian terminology, he stated, "The monad of my house is for me a mirror of the universe." (V,188). In the letter of July 27, 1759 to Kant he declined unequivocally the point of view of the physical sciences in the interpretation of reality: "Just how far man can work in the order of the world is a task for you to determine, which one should not venture to approach, however, until one understands how our soul works in the system of the little world." (I,437). Self-knowledge, then, is the one thing needful, and upon it depends everything else. "Our life is the first of all goods and the source of happiness." (I,132).

Self-knowledge, **which is not in our power apart from** knowledge of God (I,133), issues, among other things, in recognition of the basic emotionality of man. "*Optimus Maximus,*" we read in a letter to Jacobi, "demands no headaches (i.e., ratiocination) but pulse-beats." (G,V,197). Shortly after his conversion the emphasis upon the emotionality of man appears. "If the natural man has five senses, then the Christian is an instrument of ten strings, and without passions more like sounding brass than a new man." (I,393). To his brother he wrote in 1759: "Use your emotions as you use your limbs." (I,515). Again, over against the objurgations of the rationalistic Biblical exegetes with reference to the affective language of the Bible, he posed the question: "If the emotions are *members of dishonor*, do they therefore cease to be *weapons of manhood*." (H.'s italics. II,286). These and many passages like them testify to Hamann's urgent proclamation of the right of the emotions to be recognized for what they are—the gateway to the soul of man. This emphasis upon the affective elements of man's nature springs directly from Hamann's perception of the witness of Scripture to their importance. Thus it is the divine word which furnishes man with true insight into the height and depth of the emotions, their good and their evil. When Hamann sought a fitting symbol for self-knowledge with its concomitant recognition of man's emotionality, he turned to orthodox Christian theology and found it in the doctrine of Christ's descent into hell, and spoke of the "descent into the hell of self-knowledge." (II,198).

But the emotional nature of man is not the only truth which the divine word reveals about the life of feeling. Nature seen abstractly, i.e., apart from the emotions, is not really seen. "More is necessary than physics in order to interpret nature" (I,509), was the admonition to the young university teacher Kant, and with this admonition Hamann reveals his attitude toward that Newtonian physics which was for Kant so definitive. In the *Flying Letter to Nobody the Notorious* (1786), he speaks of a "violent divestiture of real objects into naked concepts and merely conceivable signs (*bloss denkbaren Merkmalen*), into pure appearances and phenomena." (VII,107). The abstracting process involves a reconceiving of natural objects which omits the emotional connotations associated with the immediate, uncritically received impression. Hence there is no real understanding of nature. For "nature is an equation of an unknown magnitude; a Hebrew word which is written merely with consonants and to which the understanding must supply the points." (I,509).

His charge against the philosophers who adopt the point of view of Newtonian physics is that "your lying philosophy has pushed nature aside" (II,281), and "the great and small Masorah has flooded the text of nature like a deluge. Was it not inevitable that all its *beauties* and *riches* become as water?" (H.'s italics. II, 285;cf.440). It is significant that these last quotations are from the *Aesthetics in a Nutshell,* in which Hamann comes to terms with the rationalistic Biblical interpretation of J. D. Michaelis[11] and his colleagues. Part of the explanation of the impassioned and eloquent nature of this work is certainly to be found in the fact that Michaelis sought to minimize the figurative and familiar language of the Scripture. Thus he minimized precisely what Hamann magnified; in so doing, Michaelis was striking at the heart of Hamann's religious philosophy.

Hamann, drawing strength from his deeply religious and at the same time aesthetic experience of Scripture, defends the parabolic form of revelation with all his considerable powers.

> Not a lyre!—nor painter's brush!—a *winnowing shovel* for my muse to sweep the *threshing-floor of* sacred literature . . . . . Poetry is the *mother-tongue* of the human race; as *gardening* is older than agriculture; *painting,* than writing; *song,*—than declamation; parables,—than deductions; barter,—than trade. (H.'s italics. II,257-258).

This subject so inspired Hamann that he rose to heights of expression unequalled almost anywhere else in his writings:

> Emotion alone gives to *abstractions* and *hypotheses* hands, feet, wings;—to *images* and *signs,* spirit life and tongue—Where are swifter *deductions*? Where is the *pealing thunder* of *eloquence* produced and its companion, *monosyllabic lightning*? (H.'s italics. II,287).

Cassirer has said of Goethe, in contrasting that poet with the mathematical physicists, that "mathematics endeavors to make all phenomena measurable, while Goethe's method wants to make them completely visible."[12] Precisely the same thing can be said of Hamann, perhaps with greater emphasis.

The restriction of the expression of truth about existence as a whole to the parabolic form implies that Hamann desired to preserve relational simplicity. Only the simplest, elemental relations may be expressed in figurative form. For greater complexity, resource must be had to analysis, and analysis always involves abstraction. It is apparent that Hamann considered the relations involved in religious and aesthetic truth to be essentially simple, no matter how grandiose the scale on which they may be drawn. "We make deductions," he wrote, "as poets, as orators and as philosophers. The former are more often closer to reason than those in the logical form. When the heart speaks, our understanding is nothing but quibbling. . . ." (I,281). In the sequel we shall examine Hamann's doctrine of relational simplicity more thoroughly. Here we may simply remark that it is a characteristic of the parabolic expression of truth.

The essential simplicity of religious and philosophic truth must, according to Hamann, be matched with simplicity of heart. In the period immediately after his conversion he prays for the "reverent simplicity of a Christian heart" (I,53), and twenty-seven years later, in the evening of his life, he still writes, "We should become children in order to enter the Kingdom of Heaven."[13] He contrasts the simplicity of the believer with the sophistication of the Enlightener. Comparing the injunction of Matthew 18:3 with the slogan of the rationalists, he says: " 'Become as children' in order to be happy—can scarcely mean: 'Have reason, clear ideas.' " (G,V,7).

Since the terms "natural language" and "abstract language" are used as key terms throughout this study, it will be well to indicate at this point what is meant by them. The term "natural language"[14] designates the historically developed vernacular of any people and likewise all poetic treatments of such a vernacular. Hamann held all language to be, in so far as it preserves its pristine nature, poetic language. By the term "poetry" Hamann meant any imaginative and affective use of a historical vernacular. As we have seen, poetry is for him the mother-tongue of the human race, and it has been hallowed as an instrument of the divine revelation. The transformation of language into a precision instrument, whether on the refined level of science or on the cruder level of professional and trade jargon, is contrasted with natural language throughout Hamann's writings. The meaning of "abstract language" for Hamann will become clearer in the subsequent pages. At present it suffices to say that it is the non-imaginative and non-affective terminology produced by the ratiocinative process.

Natural language or abstract language, poetry or mathematics—these are in Hamann's scheme the two great choices which confront the philosopher, and between which he must invariably decide. In practice, neither the ideal of pure poetry nor the ideal of pure mathematics is attainable for the philosopher, but the ideal for which he decides as his lodestar invariably guides all his thinking about the ultimate issues of life. It is the fundamental error of the abstract thinker that he holds mathematics to be the ultimate ideal of knowledge. "It seems to me," he wrote to Herder, "that the mathematicians [i.e., philosophers imbued with the mathematical spirit] are like the Samaritans: *ye do not know what ye worship.*" (H.'s italics. VI, 366). It is the spirit of "mathematical observation" which leads the philosophers astray. (IV,25). This must inevitably be so, since the great "book of nature"[15] is not written in the language of mathematics, as the physicists and their followers imagine. Mathematics cannot express the meaning of nature nor can it speak to the human heart. Goethe's dictum on this subject expresses the Hamannian thought: "Mathematics is able to eliminate no prejudice; it cannot mitigate wilfulness or allay partisan spirit; of all that is moral it can accomplish nothing."[16] Hence, it makes a very great difference whether the primordial language of nature, the language of the "firm prophetic word in the oldest documents of the human race and in the Holy Scriptures of genuine Judaism" (VII,47), or the transformed, "mutilated" language of mathematics is the medium chosen for the expression of religious and philosophic truth. Thus, form cannot be divorced from content, and, indeed, form is to a very great extent determinative of content. Only on the basis of this high estimate of form does Hamann's life-long wrestling with the problem become meaningful. For him the tyranny of words was a matter of constant concern, and he revealed his feeling about it in his phrase "the serpent's deception of language." (V,29).

The Magus' emphasis upon the language of nature as the form in which statements about the ultimate meaning of life must be cast is unusual in the history of philosophy and theology, and doubtless this emphasis accounts for his strange isolation or for what Windelband has called his "quaint singularity"[17] in the history of thought. If the emphasis upon external form would seem to prejudice his case in advance—particularly in so far as his religious philosophy is concerned—it may be profitably noted that the considerable differences between Lutheran and Calvinistic Protestantism have been ascribed precisely to the differences in the respective forms in which these two versions of essentially the same faith were originally cast. This thesis is ably expounded by Hermann Bauke in his study of Calvin's theology.[18] The material assumptions of Lutheranism and Calvinism were originally approximately the same. In this respect Calvin was the disciple of Luther. But the formal structures of the two apologetic theologies have so affected their tone that the result is two clearly distinguishable types of Christianity. Calvin was temperamentally as much of a rationalist as the high scholastics, and explicated his faith with logical rigor, whereas Luther repudiated the scholastic method as inadequate for the expression of his faith. The scholasticism of Melanchthon and his followers did not become definitive for Lutheranism simply because Luther himself, rather than his disciples, was the authoritative bearer of the Protestant spirit for the Lutheran religious community. His religion, according to Bauke, was a religion more of the heart than of the head, and it is his religion rather than that of his scholastic disciples which mediates New Testament Christianity to the majority of his followers. Whatever one's judgment upon Bauke's theory may be, it cannot be denied that he is here dealing with fundamental issues, and that in so far as this is true, we have here a corroboration of Hamann's insight that the formal expression of faith is a decisive matter.

We might note parenthetically that Hamann, whose intention to adhere to traditional Lutheranism is beyond doubt and whose striving with religious problems prompted one writer to describe him as "probably the most profound Christian thinker of the eighteenth century,"[19] would correct Bauke at this point by replacing his duality of religion of the head and religion of the heart with the duality of the language of logic and the language of nature. For, in Hamann's eyes, the religion of the heart is not at all a pauper with no definite external means, i.e., with no objective form of expression which it can call its own. Natural language is the objectively given instrument of true religion and of true philosophy. It is the "womb" (Cf.VI,39) of reason and reason's progeny, and therefore no mere rationalisms can compete with it. All rationalisms arise out of natural language and are finally accountable to it, for they must somehow be explicable in terms of it. In Hamann's words, natural language is the "mother of reason and revelation, their alpha and omega." (G,V,122). This is the point at which, we believe, Hamann still has something to say concerning the philosophy of religion. Blanke stated some years ago that the influence of evangelical Christianity upon Hamann's language philosophy needed greater appreciation than it had found up to that time.[20] This was true, and still is to some extent, but the full influence of that language philosophy on evangelical Christianity still awaits an intellectual climate suitable for its appropriation. The full scope of Hamann's idea that language is the "mother of revelation" as well as of reason needs to be understood.

"It is my same old tune," Hamann wrote, "but through language are all things made." (G,V,122). This, as we have seen, was an insight which he gained principally through his conversion by the Biblical word. Just as the world and living organisms were called into being in the beginning by the word of God, so man's spiritual life is re-created by that same word as it is spoken through the Gospel. But the power of the word to create is a characteristic not only of the divine word; it is also a characteristic of the human word, in so far as it partakes of the nature of the divine word. For Hamann, it is therefore permissible to speak of human speech as "creative energy,[21] if one remembers that the transcendent God of the Biblical revelation is the constant source of that energy for him. Hamann's concern with natural language was never a matter of purely aesthetic or belletristic interests, but a profound concern with the medium in which God had chosen to reveal himself. Prior to his conversion Hamann had subscribed to the basic tenet of the Enlightenment that reason is able to devise abstract formulas which can be utilized as norms for the regulation of life in its larger aspects.[22] With his conversion, this faith in formulas vanished forever. Language was for him not the pliable material with which abstract norms may be molded, but was a reality to be appropriated and understood,[23] as far as one may speak of understanding a living organism which one may observe, but not mutilate or destroy.

It is instructive to consider Hamann's attitude toward attempts at language reform, especially the attempt of the French Academy to keep the French language standardized and pure. Hamann had a particularly keen scent in such matters, detecting the proneness of reason to refashion language where others failed to do so. In this connection he wrote in *Miscellaneous Remarks concerning Word Order in the French Language* (1760):

> The purity of a language diminishes its riches; a too strict correctness diminishes its strength and manhood. In as large a city as Paris are foregathered *annually*, without expense, *forty* learned men who know *infallibly* what is pure and decent in their mother-tongue and what is necessary for the monopoly of this second-hand trade. Once, however, in *centuries* it happens that a *gift of Pallas—a human image—falls* from heaven, empowered to rule the public treasury of a language with wisdom—like a *Sully*, or to increase it—like a *Colbert*. (H.'s italics. II,151-152).

Bound up with this assertion are many ideas which we shall encounter in other contexts. At this juncture, however, we may note how effectively the cited passage stresses the natural process of language development, an objective process which takes place apart from the self-conscious intervention of reason. The asseveration that "the purity of a language diminishes its riches" thrusts us into the very heart of the Hamannian language philosophy. It means that a language which is deprived of its imaginative and affective force, "its strength and manhood," is impoverished. For, as he wrote in *Aesthetics in a Nutshell*: "Nature works through the senses and emotions. He who mutilates their instruments—how may such a one perceive?"[24] In Hamann's judgment, the French Academy's efforts were directed toward the mutilation of the language of nature, for it was the task of that body to preserve the stylistic forms acceptable to good taste. Thus were ruled out unusual idioms, images, tropes, and the vivid, imaginative language which Hamann himself loved so excessively.[25] The language stereotypes which good taste[26] might approve may once have been charged with imaginative and affective power, but in the course of time such power has been lost. To assert and preserve their authority in the realm of letters is to vitiate natural language, to excise its power at the root.

Hamann rejected, as we see from the cited statements, also the idea that learned men can be the arbiters of language. The reason for this is given in the statement that at intervals in history there arises a genius, "a gift of Pallas," who is able to accomplish what cannot be accomplished by the joint efforts of scholars in council, namely, to explore the unusual and unused, perhaps half-forgotten or unknown areas of natural language, i.e., "to rule the public treasury of a language with wisdom like a Sully," or to create new and effective syntheses out of the old elements, i.e., "to increase it like a Colbert." True creativeness does not issue in the creation of new words, as in the case of the philosopher with his abstractions, but in the creation of new sense-units of language, new phrases. In this way the old becomes the new; the familiar is seen in a new light. Genuine novelty and tradition combine in a most fruitful way. It is plain that he held natural language to find its greatest expression through great individuals, and that time is necessary for this development, for it occurs only "once in centuries." As there will be occasion to notice subsequently, the time process in history is a matter of great importance for Hamann, and the efforts of the rationalists to escape the necessity of a serious reckoning with it lead them into error in all areas.

Although the French Academy's undertaking involves only a modest control of language, and that in a philosophically indifferent area, nevertheless Hamann's critique of its efforts clearly reveals his attitude toward over-arching reason in its efforts to control language. In so far as the Academy's efforts to separate man from the "riches" of language and from the time-process with regard to the appearance of geniuses are concerned, the dictum which Hamann liked to apply, in one version or another, to the rationalistic philosophers applies here also: "The philosophers have always given truth a bill of divorcement in that they have separated what nature has joined together, and vice versa." (IV,45).

The attitude of the Magus toward attempts of reason to regulate language may be further inferred from his opinion of spelling-reform. In an ironical essay entitled *New Apology for the Letter "h"* (1773), Hamann took to task in most humorous fashion a minor Berlin rationalist who had objected to the retention of the silent letter "h" in certain German words. (IV, 115-147). Although his lampooning of this effort was actually a veiled attack on natural religion, it discloses his feeling toward rational intervention in language. Seven years later his objurgatory essay on Klopstock's proposed spelling-reform was in the same vein. (VI,23-44). That he was willing to take up the cudgel even against the author of the *Messias* can only be explained by reference to his feeling that something quite important was involved here. That something was not the question of proper spelling, but the assumptions which underlay such reformatory ideas. Hamann's strength as a critic did not reside in his ability to judge the details of a system, but, to use Kant's phrase concerning him, in the ability "to think things in the large."[27] Hamann saw that the question here was not one of quibbling about the minutiae of language, but of its higher purpose, which involves its meaningful use. Therefore he wrote:

> For as little as the purpose of speech consists in mere articulations and modifications of blind tones, far less still does the purpose of writing consist in an enumeration, weighing, and punctuation of their mute substitutes, which all amounts to a Pharisaic tithing of mint, anise, and cummin in relation to the true, natural, and higher purpose which unites speech as well as writing—to a shekinah, tabernacle, and chariot-throne of our thoughts, concepts, and sensations through audible and visible signs of language. To transform these material aids of our intellectual need and caprice into the final and only purpose would be the crudest abuse of poetic license and sensuality.[28]

This passage is highly characteristic of Hamann, for here we find the most prosaic of matters connected with ultimate mysteries of the religious life. Spelling-reform as "the Pharisaic tithing of mint, anise, and cummin" is contrasted with the manifestation of the divine presence in the "shekinah, tabernacle, and chariot-throne." These latter Biblical symbols are used to represent the union of word and concept or of thought and language in the process of meaning. The very fact, however, that he had recourse to the symbols of the divine-human togetherness in order to express the concept-word togetherness indicates a great deal about his feeling with regard to the process of speech. The meaning of the passage is simple. Language was created for the high purpose of conveying meaning, and that purpose should concern us more than the mechanical details of its physical actuality. Reason can tamper with the "aids" of meaning, but in so doing it does not alter the great fact of natural language and its function. But to translate Hamann's minimal meaning into more prosaic terminology is to lose not only the affective tone of his utterances, but also the important metaphysical and religious implications.

The belief that language is originally molded on reality served to encourage his innate love of linguistics, for it provided a reason for believing that the study of historical vernaculars could yield important insights into the structure of reality.[29] Actually he was an assiduous and successful student of a number of foreign tongues and a tutor of young men in two—French and English—besides instructing his son in several. Herder was his pupil in English, the study of which was begun with Shakespeare's *Hamlet*. The far-reaching implications of the first encounter of the younger Herder with this drama in the original language under the tutelage of one of the epoch-making Shakespeare-enthusiasts of the Continent is at once obvious. It was characteristic of Hamann that language instruction was the occasion for immediate encounter with the best a language has to offer; hence, it was but natural that Shakespeare was regarded as the gateway to English. In addition to the language mentioned, Hamann pursued studies in Latin, Hebrew, Arabic, Lettish, and Portuguese.[30] To be sure, his mastery of these tongues varied from thoroughness at one extreme to a merely superficial and fleeting acquaintance at the other. But with the exception of Portuguese, all of his language studies were reflections of deep cultural interests.[31] Thus it is not surprising to find him especially diligent in French studies during what one might call his Enlightenment-phase, i.e., just prior to his conversion in 1758. In addition to his intellectual concern with French, his occupation as tutor and later as translator for customs officials in Königsberg caused him to become exceedingly proficient in that language. In the period of concern with the genius-concept it is not surprising to find him interested in the mother tongue of Shakespeare, for along with Homer, Shakespeare provided the example of genius *par excellence*. Greek was, however, as Nadler remarks, "the language of his mature years and of his great thoughts."[32] This mastery of languages was not, however, without its unfortunate consequences, for, coupled with his extraordinarily wide reading, it led to all too frequent citations from foreign languages, many of which in no way serve to illuminate his thought.

Hamann translated four longer works and numerous short articles into German. Of the four longer treatises, one was translated from French and three from English. The translations are: *Des Herrn von Dangeuil Anmerkungen* (1756), done at the request of his Riga merchant-friend, J. C. Berens; *Ferdinando Warners vollständige und deutliche Beschreibung der Gicht* (1770), done for Kant and his friend, Green; *Heinrich St. Johann Vitzgraf Bolingbroke und Jakob Hervey* (1774); *Humes Gespräche über die natürliche Religion* (1780). The first three translations were done at the instigation of friends; only the last was done as a result of compelling spiritual and intellectual need; Hamann engaged Hume as an ally in his battle against the protagonists of natural religion, and this translation has to be seen as one of his tactics in that struggle. It was never published, inasmuch as another translation appeared before Hamann's was ready for press; therefore, it is of interest only to the student of Hamann. It is noteworthy that none of Hamann's translations were done for monetary gain—except the routine translations required in his job with the tax officials of Königsberg. They were done either on behalf of friends or as the result of an inner compulsion, and they bespeak not only his interest and ability in languages, but also his pure motives.

Since it was Hamann's conviction that we find the history of a people in its language (I,449), he turned to naturally developed languages for insight into the peculiarites of those who spoke them. But "no language can be understood from *books* alone," and "the *language of writers* is a dead language in relation to the *language of conversation*." (H's. italics. II,205). Hence, one must turn to the living spoken language as a guide to true comprehension of its nature. One then finds that the spoken language is characterized by richness of idiom, and it is from the peculiarity of the idiom that we gain some idea of the individual and folk mind.[33] Though interested in the mechanics of language to the extent of having started a grammar of the French language in his youth (I,345), and having written somewhat on comparative grammar (I,345), he was finally interested in language as a means of gaining access to the spirit of a people. So intimately is language bound up with life, and so faithfully does it reflect the peculiarities of the multifarious activities of man that "court, school, trade and traffic, exclusive guilds, cliques, and sects have their own dictionaries." (II,210). As a people and their activities, so are their languages and their specialized jargons.

Although great literature is the language of writers, it reflects to a considerable extent the idiom of the spoken language. Thus, in so far as it remains unmutilated by attempts at rational regulation, it provides an almost inexhaustible thesaurus, which is the rightful legacy of a people; it constitutes an important part of the "public treasury of a language." Hamann's own example proves to what extent he took this idea seriously. He drew many of his expressions from the German of Luther, particularly from his translation of the Bible, and wove them into the fabric of his thought and expression. "What *Homer* was to the ancient Sophists," he confessed, "the *Holy Books* have been to me ....." (H.'s italics. G,V,38).

Hamann's own experience with Scripture as the revelation of God through the medium of natural human speech combined with Luther's principle that theology is a *grammatica in spiritus sancti verbis occupata*[34] to impress him indelibly with natural language as the gateway to true philosophy. Thus he wrote to Jacobi in 1787:

> Do you understand now ... my language-principle of reason, and that with Luther I make all philosophy a grammar, a primer of our knowledge, an algebra and construction according to equations and abstract signs, which signify nothing *per se* and everything possible and real *per analogiam*.[35]

Going straight to the heart of the matter, he explained the differences between Jacobi—the more traditional thinker—and himself thus: "What in your language is 'being' I should prefer to call the 'word'." (G,V,516). Linguistics, then, is the basic philosophic discipline. What geometry was to the Platonic Academy, language was to Hamann.

Language evoked religious feelings in Hamann, but at the same time it stimulated his scientific curiosity. For he felt that language offered an opportunity close at hand to achieve real knowledge about human existence, an opportunity which the scientists and philosophers missed because of their concern with "celestial discoveries," and he spoke sardonically of the "spirit of mathematical observation" confined exclusively to "ethereal spheres." (IV,25). Religious motivation was always far stronger with Hamann than scientific motivation, but as even Hettner admits, his concern with language constituted a concern with science.[36] Unger well recognized this side of Hamann, and wrote that "we. . . . find a double language concept represented by Hamann, a metaphysical and an empirical, an almost mystical and a rationalistic."[37] Hence, one cannot be surprised to find the Magus characterizing genuine language philosophy as "an algebra and construction according to equations and abstract signs." But he was careful to avoid the implication that such a systematization with its abstractions was to be taken as a "copy" of reality in the sense in which the abstract formulas of the current physics were held to be such. For he plainly specifies that such an "algebra" would "signify nothing *per se* and everything possible and real *per analogiam*." It is thus revealed in what sense Hamann's "science" is to be understood.

Early in Hamann's career we find him stressing the importance of language study and even its priority over mathematics and logic in connection with intellectual development. This remained his position throughout life, and the only change which can be discerned in this connection is a deepening of the conviction that the symbols of natural language are to be taken quite seriously as clues to the nature of thought and reality. (I,159-160). Particularly relevant for our discussion at present is the stress upon the analysis of natural language for an understanding of "higher, more important, more difficult, indeed of spiritual things." (I,160).Twenty-five years later he adopts the same position with the exception that he is somewhat more specific as to the connection of natural language with reality. In writing to F. E. Lindner, whose son he was tutoring, he expresses the conviction that Latin grammar is intellectually more useful than mathematics. (VI,335). Obviously the case for traditional grammatical analysis is overstated. But it should be remembered that the Aristotelian-Alexandrian theory of grammar was unquestioned in his day. More significant is the parallel he draws between syntax and human relations. (VI,335;cf.345). The implication is that the relations subsisting between the words of natural language are to be compared with the relations between individual human beings. As we shall see at a later stage, Hamann's epistemology requires the reality of the objects of sense and of the relations subsisting between such objects, but not the reality of relations between abstract concepts. This position rules out a purely abstract analysis of human relations, because the alleged relations of abstract systems relate nothing. Only natural language, with its signs for real objects and relations between them, can act as a surrogate for real individuals and their interrelations. In connection with language study, Hamann decries mere memorizing, and emphasizes "attention" and "judgment" in its stead. (VI,345).

One weakness of Hamann lay in the fact that he who was so quick to question the abstract systems of the philosophers did not so readily question the categories of the traditional grammarians. Had he done so, his principle of the importance of the analysis of natural language would have proved itself more immediately useful. For instance, the notion that the units of ordinary language are constituted by the traditional parts of speech, i.e., the isolated words to be found in a dictionary, rather than by sense-units,[38] phrases, or sentences, he seems never to have explicitly questioned. Yet here is an excellent example of his often repeated principle that the philosophers are perennially separating that which nature has joined together. A deduction from Hamann's clearly stated general principles leads inescapably to the conclusion that not isolated words, but sense-units are the basal elements of language. For in his verbalistic philosophy all meaningful utterances require two distinct types of linguistic signs. As we shall see, these signs, subjectively conceived, represent the reflective and perceptive faculties of the mind, and, objectively conceived, they represent relations and objects. Therefore, it is possible in connection with Hamann's thought to define the sense-unit as a combination of linguistic signs representing the reflective and perceptive faculties of the mind, or, again, as a combination of linguistic signs representing relations and objects. In the light of these definitions—the essential validity of which for Hamann's thought will be established in a subsequent chapter—it may be said that the basal elements of language are the smallest possible sense-units, i.e., combinations of linguistic signs which clearly stand for either the reflective and perceptive activities of the mind or relations and objects.

Since Hamann does not admit the reality of objects except in so far as they are immediately intuited as undifferentiated wholes of ordinary human experience, only natural language is, strictly speaking, the bearer of the sense-unit. Abstract language destroys the genuine duality of language by eliminating concrete words and substituting for them reflective or relational words. Hence, as we have defined the sense-unit, it cannot properly occur in abstract language, but must be sought in natural language. From this it is obvious why the structure of natural language is decisive for Hamann. When Hamann states that language is the "organon" or "criterion" of reason,[39] he means that the structure of natural language is the norm for reason.

Hamann held that "a mind that thinks at its own expense will always interfere with language." (II,131-132). That is, the original thinker does not merely repeat the stereotypes and clichés of language, but creates expressions which may serve as more adequate vehicles of his meaning. For Hamann, this was true of both the poet and the abstract thinker, but in unequal senses. The poet, the truly creative master of language, creates new sense-units; he does not simply parrot "at the expense of a society" (II,132) the current stereotypes of his mother-tongue —"the words prescribed for him." (II,132). The poet rarely creates new individual words; instead he creates new phrases, i.e., new combinations or syntheses with the words provided for him by the language in which he composes. The abstract thinker, however, often creates new individual words, i.e., new abstractions. The creativity of the poet is genuine, that of the abstract thinker spurious. God himself is the "poet at the beginning of days" (II,282), not the primordial philosopher.

Actually it can be shown that Hamann's own procedure as a

writer was to create new sense-units which represent combinations of terms referring to objects of ordinary sensory or imaginative experience, and to avoid terms which are primarily reflective or, to use his concept, relational. The full explication of this idea must be delayed until the discussion of Chapter III concerning the duality of symbolism in all natural language.

As important as language was for Hamann, he was never able to formulate anything like an adequate definition of it. The few definitions which he offered are quite inadequate. He speaks of language, for example, as "the true art of thinking and acting or of communicating oneself and understanding and interpreting others." (VI,325-326). Further, language is the "means of communicating our thoughts and of understanding the thoughts of others." (II,128). These definitions are inadequate on two scores. First, they make no reference at all to the peculiar medium of language proper. Hence, on the basis of them no distinction between linguistic and non-linguistic signs can be made. Secondly, there is no reference to meaning in the objective sense. In these attempts at definition, he does not, of course, do justice to the insights into the nature of language almost everywhere apparent in his writings. When, however, he prefaces one of the cited definitions with the word "mathematics," contrasting it with "memory work," we have no right, as Unger does,[40] to complain of the obscurity of his meaning, for, as we have already seen, he simply desired to call attention effectively to the necessity for logical thought in the interpretation of natural language. On this interpretation, language study may be considered as a sort of "mathematics" or "practical logic." Since the structure of natural language is a better guide to the structure of reality than the language of pure mathematics or of formal logic, it may then be asserted to be the true intellectual discipline. For unlike Bergson, Hamann believed that language *is* "molded on reality."

In spite of his recognition of the tremendous difficulties involved in an understanding of language, Hamann never gave up the attempt. To be sure, the ultimate nature of language he held to be mysterious, and yet he seemed to feel that, if human reason could be effectively applied anywhere, it could be effectively applied to language. Moreover, the universal importance of language impressed him, and further added to the urgency of an understanding of its nature. In an interesting passage from the *Miscellaneous Remarks concerning Word Order in the French Language,* he says:

> Money and language are two subjects whose investigation is as profound and abstract as their use is universal. Both stand in a closer relationship than one might presume. The theory of one explains the theory of the other; therefore they seem to flow from common sources. The wealth of all human knowledge rests on the exchange of words; and it was a theologian of keen wit who declared theology—this oldest sister of the higher sciences—to be a *grammar of the language of the Holy Scriptures.* On the other hand, all the goods of civil or social life have reference to money as their *universal standard* .... (H's italics. II,135).

Language and money, economics and theology—for Hamann these things are not separate, but must be seen and understood in their togetherness. If natural language is the key to revelation and reason, money is the key to trade. Thus the visible is the gateway to the invisible, and through it one must pass, if he would reach the invisible. This is a genuinely Hamannian principle, and we shall encounter it again. It is thus seen that, when Hamann adduces a secular example, it is for the purpose of understanding the more clearly a religious principle. For it is to be remembered that language is the point at which the encounter between the divine and human takes place. It is the Logos (VII,151) in space and time.

Our investigation in this chapter has led from revelation to grammar and its philosophy. This represents a faithful following, at least in large outline, of Hamann's thought. Throughout the chapter our principal theme was the primacy of natural language. It is true that Hamann based the authority of natural language on the divine revelation. Natural language in its poetic form is the language of the spirit, because God has so ordained it in his general revelation through the poets of all races and through his special revelation to the Jews and Gentiles in the Biblical word. In the final analysis, no other reason need be given for the primacy of natural language; God's choice of it as the supreme revelatory medium is decisive for Hamann. Even an acknowledgment of the extra-Biblical revelation is dependent upon an acknowledgment of the Biblical revelation. Yet human reason can discern, to no small degree, the grounds for the choice of natural language.

Since man is an emotional as well as an intellectual being, and since his spirit is reached primarily through his emotions, the reason for the primacy of natural language in relevation is patent. For poetically uttered natural language is the language of the emotions. Why God created man as an emotional being is a secret hidden in the divine wisdom.[41]

But man's emotionality is not the only reason for the primacy of natural language. Natural language takes precedence over the specialized languages of reason, since it is the "womb" or source of them, and they are finally accountable to it. Natural language further manifests its own logic, which is the true logic, since it is genuinely natural, and since it constitutes the only link with ultimate reality. In writing to Jacobi in 1783, he added to certain remarks concerning the nature of pure reason the following words:

> I have, however, entirely given up this investigation on account of its difficulty, and now hold myself to the visible element, to the *organon* or *criterion*—I mean language. Without a word, no reason—no world. Here is the source of creation and government. (G, V, 7).

The strength of the Biblical revelation is its language, which is at once human and divine. On its human or natural side, it transforms even simple folk, "Galileans and fishermen," into wise men; but language, wrongly understand and misapplied, may transform the wise into fools. In a frequently cited and important passage from *Golgotha and Scheblimini* (1784) Hamann indicts the misuse of language thus:

> The abuse of language and of its natural testimony is the grossest *perjury*, and makes the transgressor of this first law of reason and its legitimacy the worst misanthropist, traitor, and adversary of the plain sincerity and candor upon which our dignity and felicity rest. (H.'s italics. VII, 37).

Therefore, language possesses a twofold nature, a good and an evil one. "It is the two-edged sword for all truths and lies." (G,V,122). In order to understand the abuse of the "natural testimony" of language it is necessary to see that overweening reason seeks a divorce from language, but, since this is impossible, it effects a compromise with language which undermines its validity. In the following pages we shall attempt to trace the outlines of Hamann's thought as he wrestled with the problem of the rationalistic transformation of language into a form of "perjury." It will be seen that, in Hamann's conception, the unity of language is destroyed by the excessive intervention of reason. If, as Urban says, "language is the last and deepest problem of the philosophic mind,"[42] Hamann wrestled all his mature life with the most difficult and important of philosophic problems. Hamann's peculiar contribution was his emphasis upon the primacy of natural language both for an understanding of the nature of language in general and for an understanding of the structure of experience.

## CHAPTER II

## LANGUAGE AND EXPERIENCE

In one sense, the theme of Hamann's philosophy may be summed up in his dictum: "Experience is after all always the best school and evidence the best proof." (G,V,86). For with this statement are bound up all the various skeins of his thought. But, as Whitehead well says, "the word 'experience' is one of the most deceitful in philosophy,"[1] and on its definition, we may add, hinge the important issues of any philosophic system. This entire study is, from one point of view, an extended definition of that term, and I may be excused, if I do not summarily define it here. Nevertheless, it may be said that a definition should have to make it quite clear that, for Hamann, the subjective aspects of experience always imply, at least on the human level, their objective correlates. In this chapter, where it is my task to establish that experience is for Hamann essentially verbal or linguistic, it will become plain that the parallelism of the subjective and objective aspects of experience is a basic Hamannian principle.

Hamann frequently appealed to Nicholas of Cusa's *principium coincidentiae oppositorum*, though ascribing it always to Giordano Bruno.[2] But this should not be understood to mean that he conceded the capacity of human reason to arrive at a metaphysical principle which resolves all contradictions.[3] It is my opinion that two things are involved in Hamann's appeal to this principle. First, it is a statement of the religious belief that all contradictions are resolved on the divine, not on the human level. Secondly, it is another way of Hamann's asserting the inevitable togetherness of distinct and yet naturally associated elements of experience, just as the human body and its limbs are distinct from one another and yet constitute an empirical, functional unity. (VI,20). In connection with language, the appeal to this principle is merely another way of his stating its inseparability from thought. In other words, it is a variation of his thesis that thought, though distinct from language, is inseparable from it. This interpretation is supported by the fact that Hamann cites the *principium coincidentiae oppositorum* precisely at those times when the linguistic bases of his philosophy are most apparent. Again, it can be applied to the union of the opposites, reflection and perception in cognition, and relations and objects in external experience, as that union is reflected in natural language. This, however, is a subject which belongs to another chapter. In sum, it appears that Bruno's principle meant for Hamann, on the human level, the togetherness of any of the distinct elements of human experience which may be observed in a functional union, but its most important application is to the opposite elements of language.

No matter how complex the ramifications may be, the theme of this chapter is essentially simple. It is the inseparability of thought and language for Hamann, language constituting the objective aspect of experience in contradistinction to thought as the subjective aspect. In asserting the omnipresence of some sort of linguistic symbolism in connection with thought, Hamann was asserting the dependence of all thought upon objective experience. Except from any but the strictly behaviorist point of view, language signifies a togetherness of concept and word. But as to the nature of this togetherness no general agreement has prevailed among philosophers. Thus, in treating this theme, Hamann was dealing with a most difficult but important matter. The following generalizations may help to set his ideas in their proper framework.

Most of the great philosophers have explicitly conceded that the problem of the relation of the concept to the word or of reason to language is of fundamental importance for philosophy. But their solutions of the problem differ greatly. They may, however, be divided into three types or groups. To the first group belong those who would, in the last resort, seek an escape from the fetters of language; to the second group belong those who would not seek an escape, deeming this finally impossible, but who would refashion language to render it a more precise instrument of thought; to the third group must be assigned those who accept the ineluctable union of thought and language as a fruitful marriage of inner and outer experience. Allowing for quite significant differences between the thinkers within each group, we may still consider the following in general agreement with reference to their attitude toward the language of ordinary discourse. To the first group belong Plato,[4] Plotinus, Berkeley,[5]

Bergson, and, oddly enough, certain contemporary Soviet linguists,[6] for they all hold that somehow reality or even ultimate reality may be intuited apart from language. The second group includes philosophers like Descartes,[7] Leibniz, Russell,[8] and Whitehead,[9] for these thinkers maintain that reason must refashion language in order to transform it, whether such a transformation appear in the form of an international auxiliary language, a logical calculus or a revised metaphysical vocabulary. The third and final group includes men like Hamann, Herder, Humboldt, and Cassirer, all of whom see in the togetherness of thought and language the most promising possibilities, and therefore neither search for an escape into a realm of a-lingual intuition nor wish to remold linguistic symbolism after the image of reason. Philosophers like Kant[10] who omit to deal consciously with the problem of language do not thereby escape the full force of the problem. Some interpreters have suggested that the Kantian critique of reason is in effect a critique of language. If so, nothing is gained by Kant's dealing unconsciously or indirectly with this important topic. That he failed to come to grips with the problem of language makes Hamann's criticism of him doubly interesting, for this is exactly the point at which he opens up and maintains his attack on the system of his great contemporary.

Before leaving this discussion, it is worthwhile to note that there is still another way of approaching this particular question, a way which might be described as the reverse of the Berkeleyan procedure, since it involves a radical externalization of the linguistic process. It is the conception of behaviorism, whose most important proponent in this area is John B. Watson. Behaviorism concedes the apparent problem of the relation of thought to language, but allegedly solves it by denying that we have in point of fact to do with a duality at all. Watson writes, for example, that "what the psychologists have hitherto called thought is in short nothing but talking to ourselves."[11] In this way the duality is held to disappear and the problem to be solved, for language is thus completely externalized. Obviously this is the culmination of a trend, prominent since Darwin's advent, toward assimilating man to nature scientifically conceived.[12]

Experience was for Hamann quintessentially the *word*. It

has been stated that Kant in his critical philosophy was "thinking not of the structure of language but of the structure of experience."[13] Hamann's retort to that assertion would be that language *is* experience in its most significant form. Hamann did not arrive at this principle by virtue of reflection on the nature of experience or of language in the abstract, but chiefly as the result of his conversion experience in London in 1758, when he was deeply and permanently impressed by the fact that the Biblical revelation was in the form of the word. "God reveals himself—the Creator of the world is a writer—" he wrote in the *Biblical Meditations of a Christian.* (I,56). But the remarkable thing was that God, the writer, had not chosen to write in the language of the philosophers. Rather he had condescended to write in the vernacular. (I,85-86). Hamann would no doubt have been interested in language without his religious experience. We have evidence of that from his attitude prior to his conversion,[14] but his conviction that ordinary language, which is also the language of poetry, provides the clue to an understanding of reality indubitably stems from his religious conviction.

In the course of years Hamann's conviction that natural language is the key to the understanding of reality—as far as he conceived understanding in this connection to be possible at all—deepened and broadened. He never lost the point of view which became his as a result of the conversion experience, namely, that God had chosen to ennoble human language by revealing himself in it, but in the course of time he did concern himself more and more with the purely human aspects of language. In 1768 he wrote to Herder: "I keep myself to the letter and the visible and material as to the hand of a clock:—but what is behind the dial is the art of the master craftsman. . . ." (III,381-382). That is to say, he exalts the empirical elements of experience without conceiving them to exhaust reality, but indeed to render it the more marvelous. Some fifteen years later he wrote to Jacobi: "I . . . . now hold myself to the visible element, to the *organon* or *criterion*—I mean language. Without a word, no reason—no world." In this latter quotation he asserts his point of view quite deliberately in face of the most recent developments on the philosophical scene, which principally centered around Kant's discussions in the *Critique of Pure Reason.* It is evident that Hamann was struggling to break with the purely introspective method of philosophy, i.e., to find a medium in which both reason and experience could be found in concrete form. He thought he had actually found this medium in language, and, therefore, he spoke of his own philosophy as "verbalism," a philosophy which he conceived of as a mean between the extremes of idealism and realism. (G,V,493; cf.494-495).

The expression, "without a word—no reason," may be understood to mean that reason must objectify itself in the language process or remain ineffectual. Here Hamann set himself in sharp opposition to the ancient tradition—which was essentially the standpoint of the Enlightenment[15]—that language is a veil which should be lifted to the greatest possible extent in order that reason might see the more clearly. Elsewhere he states unequivocally: "Without *language* we would have no reason. . . ." (H.'s italics VI,25). Again he holds that reason in general is dependent upon its symbolism just as special applications of reason like the mathematical disciplines are dependent upon their symbolisms. (IV,15). His most explicit statement on this subject is to the effect that: "My reason is invisible without language. . . ." (G,V,508). While thought is not to be equated with language, there is no thought, whether highly abstract or not, apart from some kind of linguistic symbolism: "Togetherness (*Geselligkeit*) is the true principle of reason and language, by means of which our sensations and representations (*Vorstellungen*) are modified" (G,V,515), and "The entire ability to think rests on language. . . ." (VII,9). It is significant that the last quotation is from Hamann's critique of the Kantian philosophy, which in his opinion, fails to take into account the importance of language for cognition. With characteristic vehemence, he summed up his view of the importance of language for reason thus: "All idle talk about reason is mere wind; language is its organon and criterion." (VI,365).

The above quotations, as well as others which might be cited,[16] are sufficient to establish the fact that Hamann held reason, or the reflective capacity of the mind, to be necessarily objectified in language. As shall become evident subsequently, his conception of the status of abstract words is additional testimony that he held to this view.

Before there can be anything like cognition, however, the objects of sensory experience, no less than the operations of reason, must be symbolized in language. Although the objects themselves are symbols of the divine wisdom and energy, they must be symbolized further in human language. Hence, Hamann could say: "Without a word—no world." Apart from the creative word of God, the world and its objects would not exist; but apart from the verbal representation of sense objects, there can be no real knowledge of the world. This is clear from a passage like the following, in which Hamann is concerned with answering Herder's thesis that human reflection, working freely, invented language:

> Every phenomenon of nature was a word—the sign, symbol, and pledge of a new, inexpressible, but all the more intimate union, communication, and community of divine energy and ideas. Everything that man heard in the beginning, saw with his eyes, contemplated, and his hands touched was a living word. With this word in his mouth and in his heart, the origin of language was as natural, as near, and as easy as child's play. (IV, 33-34).

In this passage are contained all the essential ideas of Hamann's thought on the origin of language.[17] Apropos of the present discussion is simply the notion that man apprehends the world not by means of concepts alone, but by means of the concept wedded to the word.

In speaking of the verbal representation of sense objects, Hamann was frequently moved with deep religious emotion, and therefore his language is suffused with poetic imagery. In the *Aesthetic in a Nutshell*, he waxes eloquent about the creative energy of the word:

> "*Speak that I may see thee!*—This wish was fulfilled by the creation, which is *speech to the creature* through the *creature*; for *day* unto *day* utters speech, *night* unto *night* shows knowledge. Its *line* runs through every sphere to the end of the world and its voice is heard in every dialect." (H.'s italics. II, 261).

Perhaps one of the plainest statements of his thought on this subject is the utterance that "speaking is *translating* . . . . *thoughts* into *words, things* into *names, images* into *signs*." (H.'s italics II, 262). The common ground for the inner and outer experience of man is found in language; both aspects of experience must be reflected in the word. The spirit which informs his declarations of the symbolization of the world of real objects in language is quite different from that which informs his utterances on the symbolization of reason in language. When he asserts the former, he is proclaiming a fact which moves him to the very depths of his being. When he asserts the latter, he is prophetically and often bitterly reminding the rationalists of the utter dependence of reason on language.

In the sequel we shall see that Hamann's verbalistic philosophy requires a distinction between the symbols of reason and the symbols of sense experience *within* language. For the present we shall not concern ourselves with the duality within language, but only with the duality of thought and language.

The bond of union between thought and language was for Hamann a mysterious bond with religious meaning. (I,440). He wrote that language entails "the transfer and *communicatio idiomatum* of the mental and material, of extension and sense, of body and thought." (G,V,495). Against Kant he urged that language is a "sacrament" (VII,16), i.e., the mysterious union of opposites in concrete form. These and other lines of similar[13] import stress the union of "these things so different from one another," i.e., language and thought, by means of "an incomprehensible bond."

On the basis of his religious conception of the "togetherness" of thought and language, it is understandable that Hamann protested so vigorously against the separation of the constitutive elements of the cognitive process. His conception of the union of thought and language accounts for the peculiar mixture of rational arguments with religious allusions in his dicta on the subject. In his opinion the most ambitious and important attempt to divorce thought from language in his own age was undertaken by Kant. Of this, however, we shall speak in a subsequent chapter.

According to Hamann, it is the perennial tendency of the human mind to shrink from the word, to attempt to circumvent its inevitability in one of two ways. As we have noted, there is first the mystical tendency, which seeks to penetrate to the innermost secrets of reality apart from language; secondly, there is the tendency to rework language or to refashion it after the image of reason. The latter attempt is really a compromise in that the word is retained, but it is a transformed word, and hence mutilated. According to Hamann, since the human being bears his reason within himself, he thinks to have escaped effectually from experience, or to have rendered himself autonomous. Different as their methods may be, the mystic and the rationalist have this much in common: they both feel language as a burden, and they hope by one method or another to circumvent it in order to break through "the confines of sensory experience."[19] Let us now consider more closely Hamann's estimate of these two attempts at flight from linguistically mediated experience.

No matter how frequently Hamann may verbally equate the basic elements of human experience, self, nature, and God, they are nevertheless always for him quite distinct entities. These elements are intimately associated in his thought, but never fused. The bond which most effectively links man with nature, namely, language, is at the same time a barrier. Nor is nature ever identified with God in the light of such characteristic words as these: "Heaven be thanked that there is a Being high above the stars that can say of himself: I am that I am—let everything under the moon be mutable and capricious." (VII,419;cf.G,V, 495). Finally man is never identified with divinity for there obtains "an infinite misrelation to God."[20] However intimately man is properly related to nature—conceived as verbally mediated—and through the revelational word to God, these entities must be understood as discrete and not imperceptibly blended with one another. "God, nature, and reason," he wrote, "have as intimate a relationship to one another . . . . as author, book, and reader." (G,V,22). Only in the sense in which author, book, and reader are one may we speak of the oneness of God, nature, and reason (or man). But obviously the author is not to be equated with his book, nor his book with the reader, nor the reader with the author. I emphasize these distinctions at the risk of appearing pedantic, because it is a matter of fact that distinguished interpreters have failed to recognize that Hamann unequivocally declared his belief in the utter discreteness of these entities. For example, H. A. Korff taking his lead from Unger, says that Hamann's symbolism becomes "divinity itself."[21] Now it may be said with complete confidence that this is simply not true. Revelation, as will become plain later, occurs in real time and real space, and therefore shares the relative aspects of concrete reality. But more of this later.

In the last analysis, it is the failure to recognize the distinctions mentioned above that gives rise to asseverations of Hamann's mysticism. When a commentator of the first rank like Josef Nadler interprets the Magus as one of the important bearers of the "ancient mystic" tradition of German thought, which passed through the speculative, theosophic phase of the seventeenth century,[22] he can only do so because he fails to observe that Jakob Boehme arrived at his religious knowledge by means of "direct divine illumination," and that he engaged in a study of "God in himself," whereas for Hamann the divine revelation, historically actualized in the Scriptures and in the person of Christ, is constantly interposed between God and man, and, further that God is a hidden God who has disclosed only as much of himself as necessary "for our salvation and our comfort."[23] Hamann may be described as a personal mystic[24] as opposed to the speculative mystic, but when this is asserted of him, it must be remembered that between man and ultimate reality there is a barrier which may never by lifted, even for a rare moment of insight or ecstatic elevation of feeling. His unflagging insistence upon the necessity of the objectively given revelation and his constant appeal to the doctrines of the English sensationalistic philosophers, especially Bacon and Hume, must be taken into account, when one speaks of his mysticism. If a mystic is anyone who interprets existence otherwise than as sheer matter of fact, i.e., literally, then Hamann may be said to be a mystic.[25] The formulas of logic and mathematics do not exhaust reality for him. If, however, we distinguish between those who seek the truth principally from within themselves, on the one hand, and those who seek it principally from outside themselves, on the other, describing the former as the true mystics, then mysticism cannot be predicated of him. For if his philosophy makes anything at all clear, it is that man cannot free himself from dependence upon external experience, whether for knowledge of self, nature, or God.

But the mystic is not the only thinker who seeks to avoid the necessity of constant recourse to external experience. The rationalist, motivated by other interests and possessed of other techniques, is likewise persuaded that he may divorce himself from "facts and their hated evidence." (IV,336). According to the postulates of the rationalists, reason bears within itself truth, which needs but to be unfolded to yield knowledge. Hamann charges that the excessive faith in reason in his own day stems from Descartes, Spinoza, and Wolff. But we may take Leibniz as the source of Wolffianism, and hear his words as the definitive pronouncement of the spirit of Enlightenment:

> .... It is the knowledge of necessary and eternal truth that distinguishes us from the mere animals and gives us Reason and the sciences, raising us to knowledge of ourselves and God. And it is this in us that is called the rational soul or mind.[26]
>
> . . . . . . . . . .
>
> A pretty general agreement is an indication and not a demonstration of an innate principle; but the exact and decisive proof of these principles consists in showing that their certainty comes only from what is in us. . . . .[27]

That Leibniz believed it was possible to demonstrate innate principles is evidenced not alone by his arguments,[28] but by his whole system, a system which is probably unparalleled in the history of philosophy for its confidence in that which "comes only from what is in us."

It is highly significant that Hamann formally commenced his attack on the Enlightenment in the year 1759 with the *Socratic Memoirs*. For precisely by choosing Socrates, the favorite philosophic paragon of the rationalists, he declared most effectively his purpose "to disturb others in their faith." (I,437-438). While his contemporaries—at that time even Winckelmann and Lessing are to be included—were being swept along by the flood tide of confidence in human reason, pregnant with "eternal truth," Hamann alone raised his voice in defiant protest. This protest took the form of a reinterpretation of Socrates to the eighteenth century reader. Hamann's independently rebellious attitude deeply impressed Dilthey and Troeltsch, who asked in effect how this man felt constrained, just at the time when the Enlightenment was at its zenith, to offer, like a bolt from the blue, such a challenge to the prevailing faith of the age.[29]

The Socrates limned by Hamann is no rationalist or apostle of common sense. It is the irrational or non-rational elements in the Socrates of tradition which are made to predominate. The Socratic ignorance is not a propaedeutic to a thoroughgoing rationalism, but to an archetypal exemplification of the true believer's attitude.

> The ignorance of Socrates was sensation. But between sensation and a theoretical proposition is a greater difference than between a living animal and an anatomical skeleton of the same. The old and new skeptics may wrap themselves ever so much in the lion-skin of Socratic ignorance, nevertheless they betray themselves by their *voices* and *ears*. If they know nothing, why does the world need a learned demonstration of it? (H.'s italics. II, 35).

That Socrates' awareness of his own ignorance rested on "sensation" means—as we know from Hamann's doctrines in general—that he recognized intuitively and immediately that the fullness and endless variety of external objects perceived by the five senses contrasts vividly with the original emptiness of the isolated self. Knowledge is derived not from "what is in us" but from what is without us. Here is the decisive difference between the rationalistic and the Hamannian version of Socrates. Leibniz, for example, appeals to a Platonic dialogue wherein "he introduces Socrates leading a child to abstruse truths by questions alone, without giving him any information."[30] Thus the Socratic ignorance is understood in two contradictory ways. The Hamannian Socrates is ignorant of the external world, and must therefore learn of it. The Enlightener's Socrates is ignorant of the resources within himself, and only needs the maieutic assistance of an interlocutor to transform vague knowledge into clear. The fact that at this point the Enlightener's version of Socrates is probably closer to Plato's intention in the depiction of his mentor is irrelevant. Decisive for our purposes is only Hamann's reinterpretation.

The Socratic ignorance signified for Hamann the necessity for faith. "Our own existence," he continues, "and the existence of all things outside us must be *believed* and cannot be determined in any other way." (H.'s italics. II,35). The emphasis on faith or belief is partly ascribable to the influence of Hume, whose philosophy was having its effect upon him even in the first period of his literary creativity. (G,V,506). But the influence of Hume is merely the secondary source; the primary source is to be found in the New Testament, for it was out of his newly won faith in the Biblical revelation that he drew strength for his Socratic indictment of the age.

As is to be expected, the Magus stresses the daimon or genius of Socrates, but the understanding of this influence is original with him.[31] The daimon is equated both with the Holy Spirit of Christian faith and with the creative inspiration of genius. (II,38). The Socratic daimon or genius is somehow linked with the spiritual and emotional elements in the Christian faith, and therefore Socrates belongs in a sense to the prophets. "Whoever would not tolerate Socrates among the prophets must be asked: *Who the Father of the prophets is,* and whether *our* God has not named and shown himself to be a *God of the Heathen.*" (H.'s italics. II,42).

The conception of the Socratic daimon as the influence of the divine spirit and creative genius at once provides us with a very revealing insight into the foundatons of the Hamannian philosophy. For it is the permanent annealing of religious and cultural motives in that philosophy which gives it its peculiar strength and coloring. Hamann has always been difficult to place within the traditional interpretational categories. Does he belong to the history of literature, of philosophy, or of theology? Or does he belong to all three equally? In my opinion he will always be difficult to classify because of his rare blending of religious and cultural interests in a manner which does not lead to the absorption of one into the other.[32] The relationship which we found to obtain in his thought between God, nature, and man, which involves intimate association without mutual identification, may be said to obtain here. Those who would see him primarily as a philosopher or theologian are confronted with his astounding belletristic interests and critical capacity,[33] which made him the "ferment"[34] which revived German literature in the Storm and Stress Period. Those, on the other hand, who would interpret him primarily from his literary side, are, conversely, confronted with his deep Lutheran piety and his theocentric religious philosophy; they are ever reminded by him that, "A world without God is a man without head—without heart, without vitals, without powers of reproduction." (G,V,48). At no point are we able to discern more clearly the indestructible annealing of religious and secular motives which is so characteristic of him than in his conception of the Socratic genius.

The Hamannian reinterpretation of Socrates does not signalize a retreat from the principle that knowledge is not innate in the human mind, but must be assimilated from without. A superficial understanding of the genius-doctrine may see Hamann as simply shifting the source of creative power from the intellect, i.e., from the "rules of art" as intellection, to the realm of emotion or feeling. If such were the case, the source of creative power would still be within the individual and Hamann's strictures against the solipsism of the rationalists would be unjustified. But the poetic genius is as dependent upon objective experience as the scientist and philosopher. The particular form of experience upon which he is dependent, however, is the spiritual experience of mankind as crystallized in natural language. The possessor of genius, a Homer or a Shakespeare, does not have to know the rules of art, which are always contrived "after him," i.e., on the basis of his accomplished work, but freedom from rules does not mean that he can remain unacquainted with the spirit of his race as reflected in the "public treasury of a language." Apart from this treasury, he is, creatively speaking, poverty stricken. He must approach his mother tongue as a believer, as one who believes that "we find the history of a people in its language" (I,449), and that God has revealed himself in history as well as in the Biblical record. (I,138). Therefore, it is the task of the poetic genius to explore the hidden and manifold riches of his mother tongue, and out of these to create new linguistic forms which provide the vehicle of his message. (I,119). Such forms are not artificial. The abstract philosopher is a creator of new linguistic forms also, but in his case the new forms are principally new *words*, i.e., new abstract terms. "A mind which does its own thinking will always interfere with language." The religious and poetic genius, however, interferes with language in a legitimate way. He creates new phrases, new sense units—rarely new individual words—out of the material furnished by experience, out of the public treasury of a language.[35] It is the task of genius to create the right combinations of symbols from natural language, not to invent new individual symbols. (Cf. II, 131,148). But in the final resort the secret of genius is unfathomable. Socrates was given to the Greeks "by the gods" (II,42), and the genius always falls from heaven. (II,151). But the divine origin of the genius does not exempt him from dependence upon external experience.

The discussion of the creativity of genius is for Hamann far more than merely a matter of aesthetic theory. It strikes at the very heart of the subject under consideration. "Poetry," he urged against the rationalistic critics of the Bible, "is the *mother-tongue* of the human race." (H.'s italics. R,II,258). And God is the "poet of the beginning of days" (II,282), and not a cosmic mathematician, logician or moralist. It is patent that we are here dealing with the central theme of the Hamannian religious philosophy. God's word to man in the Biblical revelation is the poetic word. This does not mean that revelation is reduced to a form of human creativity, but simply that God chose to reveal himself in the language of the poets and not in the language of the abstract philosophers.

The evidence adduced suffices, I believe, to establish that in Hamann's eyes there is no genuine cognition apart from language. Experience is more than language, but this "more" cannot be rendered cognitively effective apart from linguistic symbolization. On the whole, Hamann is faithful to the notion that there is no such thing as purely "private" knowledge, i.e., private in the sense that it cannot be symbolically represented.[36]

Hamann's thought concerning the symbolic nature of all knowledge is best summed up in his remark in *The Wise Men from the East at Bethlehem* (1760) to the effect that "human living seems to consist of a series of symbolic actions by means of which our soul is capable of revealing its *invisible* nature, and produces and communicates beyond itself an *intuitive* [i.e., empirical] knowledge of its effective existence." (H.'s italics. II,156-157). This statement is explicit warranty of the fact, everywhere implied in his thought, that symbolization is the essence of mind. He recognizes that language is not the only symbolic medium available to man, but it is the most effective and important. This is true because God is a speaking God, and man, in so far as he preserves the divine image,[37] seeks to know mediately or symbolically, and not immediately or a-symbolically.

CHAPTER III

THE DUALITY IN UNITY OF LANGUAGE

In the previous chapter it was found that thought and language are inseparable for Hamann. Thus it is possible to speak of a duality of the concept and word or of thought and language, a duality which is transcended in an ultimately mysterious unity which Hamann terms the "sacrament of language." Hamannian scholarship has largely contented itself with the explication of this idea, adding the general information that Hamann held abstract language to be disruptive of the natural adhesion of language to experience. In the words of Metzke, "First abstraction, first the *ratio* artificially dissolved this original concrete unity in order to give out the abstract parts as the truth."[1] The manner in which this process takes place is generally not explicated.[2] A writer like Metzke, however, fully recognizes the importance of the subject.[3] On the other hand, Unger, whose interpretation of Hamann's language philosophy is still authoritative for many, reduces Hamann's thought to mere *attitude* rather than recognizing it for what it is, namely, a very trenchant, if sometimes hesitating critique of abstraction and the entire rational process. Thus Unger interprets Hamann, at least in this regard, as a pure romantic, and says, in effect, what Santayana has said of the romantic: ". . . . he can say nothing that is worth carrying away; everything in him is attitude and nothing achievement."[4] That such an opinion of Hamann's language philosophy is erroneous the following pages are intended to show. It is my conviction that there are hitherto unutilized resources in Hamann's writings for the illumination of his thought concerning abstractions, a matter which lies at the very heart of his philosophy, and apart from which his idea of unity is quite incomprehensible.

In an earlier chapter it was stated that the basal elements of natural language are for Hamann sense-units, which were defined as combinations of linguistic signs representing the reflective and perceptive faculties of the mind or relations and objects. Anything less than a unit which manifests these two properties is a fictitious element of language, hence of thought. The proof of the validity of this conception was necessarily delayed until the present discussion. We shall now proceed to examine the evidence that this conception is genuinely Hamannian.

The most important clues to a deeper understanding of the language philosophy are to be found in Hamann's linking of abstractions with relations, in his assumption of the reality of relations between real objects (but not between abstract entities) and in his general, qualified relativism. One shall not expect a systematic development of a theory of relations from a writer like Hamann. For, if it be true that most metaphysics since Spinoza has been characterized by the failure to recognize the importance of relations,[5] it is indeed surprising that Hamann dealt with the subject at all.

One thing is quite clear, and it is of fundamental importance for our study: Hamann frequently identified abstract substantives as expanded relational symbols, particularly in his latter days in the letters to Jacobi. For example, in the letter of April 29, 1787 he wrote to his friend, "Being, faith, and reason [abstractly conceived] are mere relations which may not be handled absolutely; they are no things, but purely scholastic conceptions, signs for understanding, not admiring (*Zeichen zum Verstehen nicht Bewundern*), aids to arouse and to hold our attention (*Hilfsmittel unsere Aufmerksamkeit zu erwecken und zu fesseln*). ...." (G,V,513). In this characterization of abstractions we are confronted with the peculiarly Hamannian interpretation: abstractions are considered as "mere relations," and are not criticized as mere qualities with a subjective status. In asserting that abstractions are signs for understanding not admiring, he passes judgment on the incapacity of abstractions to appeal to the whole man, i.e., to the emotions as well as to the intellect. He further says: "Existence [i.e. concrete existence in a world of real objects] is realism and must be believed; relations are idealism and rest upon connective and discriminatory procedure (*beruhn auf Verknüpfungs—und Unterscheidungsart*)." (G,V, 507). In this case, Hamann stresses the necessity for faith in the reception of sensory impressions of the outside world, but at the same time defines reflection, which he terms "idealism," as essentially connective and discriminatory procedure. The statement that "relations are idealism" does not mean that he denied the reality of relations proper, but that only when relations are expanded into abstractions and further relations are predicated of them, do they constitute mere relations. Hamann recognized that connective and discriminatory procedure is necessary for all language, but deplored the predominance of its peculiar symbolism in abstract language as involving a dangerous imbalance of language.

Elsewhere Hamann singles out the concept "being-in-itself," and asserts it to be "the most abstract relation" or the "most general relation, whose existence and qualities must be believed." (G,V,509). But belief in the reality of such abstract entities is an illusion, for he asks, "are there for relative concepts absolute things?" The answer is emphatically negative. (G,V. 516-517). Hamann compares the veridical nature of the word of everyday experience, which is at once the revealed word, the word which Adam had "in his mouth and in his heart" with the abstract language of the philosophers. From his criticism of the Kantian system we have the following lines:

> Metaphysics misuses the word-signs and figures of speech of our empirical knowledge as pure hieroglyphs and types of ideal relations, and works over by means of this learned mischief the *straightforwardness* of language into such a hot, unstable, indefinite something $=$ x, that nothing remains but the soughing of the wind, a magic phantasmagoria at the most, as the wise Helvetius says, the talisman and rosary of a transcendental, superstitious belief in *entia rationis*, its empty bags, and slogan. (H.'s italics. VII, 8).

The words "pure hieroglyphs and types of ideal relations" (*lauter Hieroglyphen und Typen idealischer Verhältnisse*) might even be taken as Hamann's definition of purely abstract terms. How fruitful this characterization of abstraction as a "working over" (*verarbeiten*) of the "straightforwardness of language" (*die Biederkeit der Sprache*) may be will become evident. It is informative that Kantian transcendentalism is equated with a "superstitious belief in *entia rationis*."

Relations seem to be real for Hamann in so far as they subsist between real objects.[6] They become unreal, when they are predicated of ideal entities or abstractions. In his strictures against abstractions as mere relations, he is not objecting to the reality of relations, but to their elevation to the status of objects which require further relations. Natural language must deal in relations as well as objects; indeed it is one of the principal uses of language to reveal the true nature of relations between real objects, and the master of language is he who can so use it as to disclose true relations. Thus,

> our concepts of things are mutable by means of a new language, by means of new signs which make us aware of new relations or rather restore the oldest, original, true ones. (G, V, 494).

Certain abstractions are justified, but they may not be arbitrary or derived from a purely mechanical conception of nature.[7] Further, they are to be clearly understood as mere "signs for understanding. . . . aids to arouse and to hold our attention," and not as symbols of real entities. "The real remains, the ideal depends more on us, and is mutable by means of nominalism." (G,V, 494). Thus Hamann is correctly described as a nominalist,[8] though strictly speaking he should not have been, since he admits the reality of relations, and relations are universals.[9]

Yet Hamann is not the only philosopher caught in this dilemma, as the long history of the debate over the reality of universals abundantly testifies. It is simply our concern to note that he links abstractions with relations, and indeed interprets them as standing for "mere relations." If he had criticized them as representing mere qualities, subjectively conceived, he might have been led into Berkeleyan idealism. Therefore, if we are to speak of Hamann's nominalism, it must be remembered that he does not criticize abstractions on the basis of the subjectivity of qualities. This fact is sufficient to distinguish him from the classic nominalists of the eighteenth century. Hamann would seem to say that there are only two genuinely empirical types of knowledge: knowledge of objects and knowledge of relations. The knowledge of qualities is less sure than knowledge of relations, for relations can be known apart from qualities, but qualities cannot be known apart from relations. When we assert anything of an object, we are really asserting something about its relations, but tend to think we are asserting something about its inner nature. This type of thinking is justified with reference to real objects, but not with reference to pure abstractions, in the case of which we have mere relations. The foregoing statement is somewhat conjectural, but seems to be a fairly faithful summary of Hamann's thought processes in this connection.

It is not at all conjectural, however, to assert that Hamann held to the reality of objects and the reality of relations between them. His empiricism can be understood only on this basis. That it is radical empiricism is obvious from the fact that he remains, in so far as he asserts anything on the basis of reason alone, close to demonstrable realities. And according to Russell, it is possible to demonstrate the reality of relations.[10] It has already been noted that Hamann denied that there are such entities as the universals represented by substantives. That the status of adjectives is also questionable is indicated by his statement:

> Good and evil are really general concepts which do no more than indicate a relation of ourselves to other objects and the reciprocal relation of these to us, if I may so speak. We thus stand in connection with other things and on this *nexus* is based not only our true being and real nature, but also all changes and nuances of which it is capable. (I, 139-140).

The terms "good" and "evil" are adjectival in form in the original language of this quotation (*gut und böse*). In the Hamannian thought, adjectives are thus considered as indicating relations. We may infer from his treatment of substantives that they may either be veridical or not, i.e., they may indicate true relations or imaginary ones. That relations and objects are real, when empirically demonstrable, will be seen from what follows.

If abstractions are the expanded symbolism of relations, what, we may ask, are the legitimate symbols of relations in natural language? With the exception of adjectives, which apparently may or may not be genuinely relational symbolism, it is not possible to answer this question on the basis of what he has explicity stated. The answer must be sought by deduction from his general principles. Before the attempt is made, however, it will be necessary to consider the evidence for the reality of relations and objects in the Hamannian epistemology. For it is only on the basis of the general duality of meaning in natural language that Hamann's notion of the union of discrete elements within natural language is comprehensible.

Evidence that Hamann considered relations to be real may

be had from his view of the fundamental relations of time and space. While his doctrines in this area are inchoate, as Metzke indicates,[11] the major outlines are distinct, and they establish a fundamental difference between the Magus and Kant.

Ida Axelrod, in stating that for Hamann there is "in reality .... neither past nor future, only the present"[12] is in error. In the *Metacritique of the Purism of Pure Reason* Hamann revealed that he considered time and space as objective in nature and that even the concepts of time and space are experientially derived. He suggests there that the sense of time arose from the cadence of music and the perceptible (*fühlbar*) rhythm of the heart-beat as well as from the rhythm of breathing. (VII,10). These together he considers as forming the prototype (*Urbild*) of time-measurement (*Zeitmass*) and its numerical relations (*Zahlverhältnisse*). Space, likewise, is a concept derived from experience. This he holds to have arisen from writing in its oldest form —painting and drawing—which concerns itself with the "economy of space, its delineation and determinations by means of figures." (VII,10). Thus, time is mediated through the sense of hearing and space through the sense of sight. But these concepts, having once arisen from without, were rendered "as universal and necessary as light and air for eye, ear, and voice, so that space and time, if not *ideae innatae*, at least appear to be *matrices* of all intuitive knowledge."[13]

This is a plain statement of the objectivity of time and space, for it reverses the Kantian process by making even the conceptions of time and space initially dependent upon experience. Thus perceptual time is the presupposition of conceptual time. Time and space merely *appear* to be the "matrices" of intuition. (Cf. VII,15-16). This position is consonant with his general epistemological orientation, for "*sensus* is the principle of all *intellectus*." (G,V,15). That Miss Axelrod ascribes to Hamann the doctrine of the subjectivity of time is traceable, it seems, to her erroneous identification of God with his creation. Creation is in time, but God is not. (I,122-123). There is no possibility of overcoming time within creaturely existence in the Hamannian philosophy. He adopted neither the position of the rationalists, which involves an escape from time by means of "eternal truth"

(VII,41), nor that of the mystic which admits the penetration of a "Yonder," where there is "no change or progress."[14]

It is characteristic of the Magus' approach to reality that the subject of time is dealt with directly or indirectly much more frequently than the subject of space.[15] This fact naturally flows from his non-mathematical conception of reality. For in the history of philosophy the notion of space as central has always been linked with the mathematico-logical approach to total reality. Spinoza is perhaps the best example of a thinker for whom space is of central importance, since it is with him an attribute of substance, and substance is in the final resort divine. Spinoza's immanentism is the antipode of Hamann's supernaturalism, and the contradictory evaluations of the notions of space and substance by these two thinkers flow from their fundamentally divergent philosophical presuppositions. But if Hamann omits to deal extensively with the subject of space, he counterbalances that omission with frequent, though not theoretically developed utterances, on the reality of time.

"Everything has its time" (I,356), and "everything will come in its time,"[16] are typical statements of the importance of the time-process. But not only is there a right time for everything, there is also a "wrong time" (*Unzeit*). (I,394). Time teaches us, since it reveals the true nature of earthly existence. As Metzke says "time has everything in its power,"[17] or again, in Hamann's own words, it "conquers, but also fulfills everything." (III, 125). Hamann invokes Socrates to exemplify the wise man's attitude toward the reality of the time-process. (II,22).

To gather all the evidence for Hamann's view of the reality of time would warrant an extended special study in itself. Metzke has collected a large number of the general statements apropos of the reality of time.[18] But additional important evidence is to be sought in Hamann's attitude toward the historical or time-conditioned process in connection with the development of the human spirit and intellect. Attention has already been called to the fact that language is dependent on the time-process for its growth: the genius arises from time to time to contribute to the salutary development of language. But not only the language of ordinary discourse and poetry is dependent upon the temporal process; even the language of the philosophers and the discussions bound up with it are temporal and historical for Hamann. "This much is certain, that without Berkeley there would have been no Hume, just as without the latter there would be no Kant." (VI, 244). Thus, the line of development is Berkeley-Hume-Kant; there is no line from Kant directly back to Berkeley, but only through the mediation of Hume. Hume's precedence of Kant is not merely temporal, for he exerted a great influence on Kant. It is both temporal and causal. A philosophy disposed to deal in "timeless" ideas would be forced to admit the crucial importance of the temporal-historical process in this type of development.

Even revelation is in space and time and cannot be abstracted from its historical framework. Hamann makes this clear in *Golgotha and Scheblimini,* written in answer to Mendelssohn's *Jerusalem.* Mendelssohn had sought to establish the thesis that Judaism, in contradistinction to Christianity, is no religion of dogma, but a religion of "nature and thing."[19] Judaism is reduced to revealed law, which is reasonable in itself. In other words, Mendelssohn subjects Judaism to a typically deistic reinterpretation. In answer to the proposition that Judaism is thereby distinguished from Christianity, Hamann wrote:

> The characteristic difference between Judaism and Christianity concerns therefore neither *immediate* nor *mediate revelation* in the sense in which this is taken by Jews and naturalists—nor *eternal truths* and *dogmas*—nor *ceremonial* and *moral laws,* but simply *temporal historical truths* which occurred at one time, and shall never return—*facts,* which through a confluence of causes and effects, became true at one point of time and in one place, and therefore can be conceived as true only from this point of time and space . . . . (H.'s italics. VII, 43).

Elsewhere in the same writing Hamann disclaims knowledge of "eternal truths" but admits "constantly temporal" truths. (VII, 41). The historical truths of revelation are thus both temporal and eternal. (VII, 57). Just as the development of language and literature is dependent upon the time process and the geniuses which it provides, so is revelation dependent upon the appearance of the prophet and teacher, whose advent cannot be predicted. This view of the necessity of dependence upon the temporal-historical process is, of course, the classic Christian conception.

For those who, like Hamann, accept it as a basic principle it implies that there is no escape into the realm of purely timeless truth, and that the life of the spirit may, to that extent, be said to be time-conditioned.

Though time and space are indubitably real for Hamann, they are not real in the sense in which objects of everyday experience are real. This fact renders it difficult to deal with his thought in terms of the subject-object dualism.[20] Relations have for him an objective or quasi-objective status as long as they are predicated of objects of immediate experience. When, however, they are transformed into abstractions, and further relations are asserted of them, we have, according to the Hamannian conception, mere relations of relations, statements concerning which are entirely subjective. "This and that philosophy," he complains, "is always separating things which cannot be separated at all. Things without relations, relations without things." (G,V,515).

Just what Hamann had in mind in the reference to "things without relations," unless it was an all-pervading substance like that of Spinoza, which has no need of relations, since it comprises everything, or the monads of Leibniz, which are "windowless," and are therefore incapable of relations, except in so far as they appear to have them by virtue of preëstablished harmony, is difficult to see. However, it is patent that the description "relations without things" refers to abstract systems in general, for, as we have seen, Hamann holds abstractions to be "mere relations," construed as real entities, but which are actually "fancies."

The subject-object dualism has, then, a limited usefulness in the interpretation of Hamann's epistemology. First, it is a dualism in terms of which he criticizes preëminently the form of philosophical systems. Philosophy cast in abstract form is subjective; philosophy cast in poetic form is objective. Secondly, this dualism may be of assistance in criticizing Hamann's thought, if it is clearly understood that both mind and experience have a dual nature—the former being divided into reflective and perceptive faculties and the latter into relations and objects—but that they may in turn have a dyadic relation to one another. From our study of the previous chapter we have already the clue to the nature of the relation of mind to experience in the relation of thought to language. There we found that Hamann has no rationalistic theory of the togetherness of these elements, but that it is for him simply a given fact of experience and, as such, a matter of faith.

Actually it is best to avoid the subject-object dualism in the general interpretation of Hamann's thought (except in so far as his critiques of other systems are concerned) for his constant appeal to language, in which he conceived the two modes of reality, the relational and the objective, to be symbolically present, leaves no room for its practical application. Only when reason "mutilates" language does he conceive subjectivity to be in evidence. It should be remembered that Hamann, unlike Kant, was always thinking of the structure of language, not of the structure of experience in divorce from language. The two aspects of reality become visible in linguistic symbolism. Since they cannot be separated, "there are no absolute creatures and, just as little, absolute certainty." (G,V,515). In other words, the structure of natural language tells us that there are two modes of reality, and that they must always be considered together. Neither can stand alone. It will be found that Hamann's indictment that the philosophers are frequently guilty of dealing with "things without relations," on the one hand, and with "relations without things," on the other, is susceptible of a graphic illustration from the linguistic viewpoint. This, indeed, constitutes the most remarkable aspect of the Hamannian verbalistic philosophy. But to this we shall return later.

Although it is sufficient for our purpose to establish the reality of the fundamental relations of space and time in Hamann's thought, it may be pointed out briefly that further evidence for the reality of relations in his philosophy could be adduced in the form of his general relativism. It is indeed striking that as profound a believer in the transcendence of ultimate reality as Hamann could nevertheless adopt a philosophy of historical relativism. Blanke has commented on his acceptance of a relativistic and yet at the same time absolutistic view of the Bible.[21] Unger, likewise, has recognized the peculiar combination of absolutism and relativism in Hamann's philosophy of history.[22] Relativism was an important philological and literary principle with Hamann. The relative nature of language should, in his opinion, be recognized; it is, to a certain extent, conditioned by the circumstances of its development; therefore, "in the language of a people we find its history." (I,449). The influence of the psychological and environmental conditions shaping an author's work should be taken into consideration, for "intention, time, and place of an author are all determinants of his expression." (II,210; cf. 32). Thus, the reader should identify himself as far as possible with the author in order fully to appreciate his work. This idea was so completely accepted even by the young Hamann that he pleaded for its acceptance in connection with the reading of the Bible. (I,54). From the little that has been said in this connection, it is plain that Hamann is thoroughly modern in his espousal of the principle of historical relativism. His association of this principle with absolute transcendentism differentiates him, to be sure, from the typical relativist, and renders his thought logically contradictory. A frank recognition of the dichotomous nature of his thought in this connection is necessary.

On the philosophical level, Hamann never admitted the possibility that one idea can illuminate all areas of human experience. "Our thoughts are nothing but fragments. For we know in part" (I,129), he declared early in his career, and he never wavered in this conviction. From this tenet stemmed his passionate antipathy for the philosophic systematizers. For him, metaphysical monism was, of all the errors of the intellect, the greatest and most disastrous. It may be said with assurance that Brunner, in expressing his own judgment that monism is to be equated with "monomania,"[23] was also expressing Hamann's judgment in the matter. It is most interesting to notice how the Magus, who so frequently poured out his scorn on those who claim to proceed on the basis of pure logic, turns upon Spinoza's monism with unassailable logic:

> In the first formula of Spinoza, *causa sui*, lies the whole error of the logomachy. A relative *terminus* may not, according to its very nature be conceived absolutely, without its *correlatum*. Thus (*effectus*) *causa sui* is at the same time (*causa*) *effectus sui*. A father who is his own son, and a son who is his own father. Does the whole of nature yield such an example? Spinozism is therefore an unnatural opinion, according to which nothing more than a single existing thing, which is cause and effect at the same time, is assumed. . . . .[24]

In this analysis of Spinoza's idea of "cause of itself" Hamann calls attention to the confusion of relations involved rather than explicitly invoking the law of contradiction. He points out that the term "cause" is meaningful only when its correlative term "effect" is understood. Unlike a proper name, for instance, whose meaning is dependent upon a contingently existing entity, the abstract terms "cause" and "effect" are, by definition, statements about relations in space and time. If the accepted meaning of the terms is retained, cause must precede effect. The same is true of the terms "father" and "son." By substituting the more familiar terms for the less familiar ones, he renders vivid the Spinozistic procedure in dealing with relational terminology at this important point. For the absurdity of a father who is his own son is more immediately apparent than a cause which is its own effect. According to Hamann, the greater degree of abstraction inhering in the terms "cause" and "effect" than in the terms "father" and "son' does not absolve the first set of terms of the necessity of conforming to simple logic. This, indeed, is the old error of the rationalistic system-builders; it is the attempt to conceive a relative *terminus* as if it were absolute. As we have seen, Hamann accepted Bruno's principle of the coincidence of opposites, conceiving it in his own way, but he recognized that it transcends reason. For him the coincidence of opposites was a confession of faith; for Spinoza, Hamann asserts in effect, it became the corner-stone of an allegedly rational theology. But this theology demands a single, all-embracing substance or "thing" which dispenses with relations, since it comprises everything to which it might appear to be related.[25] It would be misleading to suggest that Hamann's comments upon the philosophic systems are often as clear as the passage cited above. In fact, they seldom are. But it is important to recognize that he who is so often described as an "irrationalist" was at times capable of purely rational analysis.

The reality of relations for Hamann is nowhere more strongly attested than in his conception of self-knowledge. Self-knowledge might easily be supposed to be immediate and certain apart from any external reference, as in the case of Descartes, who held the proposition "I think, hence I am" to be "so certain and of such evidence that no ground of doubt could be alleged by the sceptics capable of shaking it."[26] In direct contradiction of this doctrine,[27] Hamann held that knowledge of self can only be determined in relation to the external realities, God and man. "God and my neighbor belong. . . . to my self-knowledge and my self-love." (I,135). Again he describes one's neighbor as the mirror of self. (I,135; ct. G,V,233). In order to know the self it is necessary to know one's relations to others. "When I desire to fathom myself, it is not a question alone of knowing what man is, but also what his status is. Are you free or a slave? Are you a minor, an orphan, a widow, and how do you stand in respect of higher beings?" (I,134). Thus at the very point where the isolated individual might find his most certain knowledge, Hamann emphatically proclaims the necessity for relations. Indeed his emphasis upon relations in human society is so great that, with a systematic thinker, it would lead to theoretical difficulties.[28] "Thus everything in the world hangs together," he said to Herder, "by means of threads which cannot be sundered without hurting us or others." (VI,71-72; cf. I,131-132). In fact he goes so far as to say that all things are so interrelated that "I cannot move from the spot, but am almost *petrified*." He invokes God as the one alone capable of altering relationships. (H.'s italics. G,V,484).

Likewise on the ethical level Hamann admitted no absolute ideals. "Good and evil indicate a relation of ourselves to other objects and the reciprocal relation of these to ourselves. . . . ." (I, 139; cf 319). Therefore, good and evil are for Hamann not qualities which inhere in the nature of persons and objects, but our employment of such terms is simply a mode of stating relations to the human and non-human environment. Therefore, all moral absolutism is entangled in the same error as all other absolutisms, namely, in the error of treating relative concepts as absolute. Influenced as he was by Pietism, Hamann refused to accept the conventional Pietistic moralism.[29] The Kantian idea of the good will he repudiated on the grounds that good will belongs alone to God, not to man. (G,V,443). "What a fine counterpart good will is to pure reason!" he exclaimed to Jacobi. (G,V, 364). In his interesting association with the Princess Gallitzin in the last year of his life, Hamann, according to her own testimony courageously pointed out to her the pride which was bound up with her religious perfectionism.[30]

Having examined the evidence for the reality of relations in Hamann's philosophy, we may now turn to his idea of the reality of objects.

Hamann recognizes a world of real objects (*Gegenstände*), which he accepts "with naive confidence in the reliability of sensory experience."[31] "The certainty of our knowledge," he asserts, "is not dependent upon our powers nor upon its organization, but for the most part on the certainly of the object itself. . . . ." (G,V,51). Here Hamann is seen to reject both pre-Kantian and Kantian rationalism, for he does hold knowledge to be primarily dependent on ratiocination, as in the case of Wolff,[32] nor does he question the testimony of the senses, as in the case of Kant.[33] Thus he exalts perception at the expense of reflection, and with this procedure is bound up a suppression of abstraction as involving a misuse of the symbolism of relations, since in his view it adds nothing to the certainty of knowledge and subtracts from its effectiveness.

In so far as it is possible to assign Hamann to a specific epistemological tradition, he must be seen as standing in the nominalistic tradition of Bacon, Hobbes, Locke, and Hume. Of these men, however, the last named was by far the most important influence on his thinking, since he afforded Hamann philosophic ground for serious reflection upon faith as a way of knowing and at the same time a point of departure for his attacks on rationalism. "I was *full* of Hume," he confessed in a letter to Jacobi, "when I wrote the *Socratic Memoirs* and the following passage of my little book has reference to that: '*Our own existence and the existence of all things* outside us must be *believed*, and can in no other way be determined.' "[34] Hamann not only began his formal attack on the Enlightenment with Hume as an ally, but until the end he considered the English philosopher the most realistic of contemporary epistemologists. After the appearance of Kant's *Critique of Pure Reason,* Hamann wrote immediately to Herder:

> Hume is always my man, because he at least has ennobled the principle of faith and included it in his system. Our countryman [Kant] is always rehashing his blustering about causality. That doesn't appear honest to me. (VI, 187).

There are, of course, significant differences between Hume and Hamann, and the latter was quick to recognize and acknowledge these differences. As early as 1759 he had written to Kant:

> The Attic philosopher Hume finds faith necessary, if he desires to eat an egg and drink a glass of water. . . . . If he finds faith necessary for eating and drinking, why does he deny his own principle, when he judges higher things than sensual eating and drinking! (I, 442; cf. VI, 187).

Hamann's translation of Hume's *Dialogues concerning Natural Religion* in 1780 is evidence of his high estimate of the philosophical worth of Hume, despite the differences between the English thinker's views and his own. It was Hamann's conviction that faith "belongs to the *natural conditions* of our cognitive powers, to the *basic motives* of our soul" (H.'s italics. VI,326), and in Hume he found a contemporary thinker of the first rank who in a sense supported him in this opinion.

Hamann accepted the proposition of the sensationalists that all knowledge derives ultimately from sources outside the mind. "There is nothing in our *understanding*," he asserted, "without having previously been in our *senses*." (H.'s italics. VI,44). By "senses" he meant the five physical senses of the body, for, as he stated in this connection: "Upon what is all knowledge based? Upon five barley loaves,[35] upon five senses which we possess in common with the unreasoning brutes." (I,127). His writings are studded with declarations of the superiority of empirical over rational knowledge. Thus he exclaims: "Should not sense knowledge be more apodictic than rational knowledge!" (G,V,504). Further: "One must begin . . . . the matter *a posteriori*, not *a priori*, which is a great mistake of the other philosophers." (G,V,232). Against Kant the watchword was essentially the same as against the orthodox rationalists of the Enlightenment: "I desire. . . . to oppose *experience to pure reason*." (H.'s italics, G,V,494). In his reckoning with rationalism, he accepted in uncritical fashion the doctrines of the empiricists in so far as they served his purposes. Their strictures against rationalism he applauded; the same strictures applied to faith in Christianity he repudiated.

Up to this point we have been engaged in showing that abstract substantives as well as adjectives denote relations for Hamann, and that in his epistemology both relations and objects are real. It is obvious that certain words of ordinary language act as surrogates for empirical objects, but the question remains as to which words of ordinary language, apart from abstract substantives and adjectives, whose status is controversial, unambiguously refer to relations. If certain words or symbols can be identified as relational in reference, whereas others clearly refer to objects, the Hamannian principle that language is a functional union of two discrete elements will receive additional light. Moreover, light is thereby thrown on his theory of abstractions.

If it is assumed that the so-called "empty or colorless ('pale') words or auxiliaries"[36] of ordinary language unambiguously refer to relations,[37] some of which are always present in linguistic expressions, either implicity or explicitly, Hamann's dicta on the unity of language take on new meaning. For instance, the idea that language involves a "transfer and *communicatio idiomatum* of the mental and material, of extension and sense, of body and thought" may be understood in a different sense from that which we have previously taken it to have. For previously this type of statement was adduced to give evidence of his assertion of the union of thought with language in general. It is my opinion, however, that Hamann often had a double meaning in mind, though unconsciously, when making assertions of this kind. Another statement of the same import maintains that language is a union of "thoughts, concepts, and sensations by means of the audible and visible signs of language." (VI,34-35). In such a case the implication seems to be that there is a demonstrable distinction between the signs of thoughts and concepts, on the one hand, and of sensations, on the other. Again language is described as the "finest parable of the hypostatic union of the sensory and rational natures, of the common idiom-exchange of their powers" (VII,12), which may likewise be taken to point to his double meaning. The fact that Hamann does not free himself in these quotations from the subject-object dualism does not vitiate the principle we have stated as definitive for his epistemology, namely, that both relations and objects are real. It should be remembered that he had to make a distinction somehow, and that the terminology for any other distinctions was not available to him.

If, as I believe, the archetype of Hamann's abstract relational symbolism is to be sought in the so-called empty words and syntactical devices of ordinary language, the application of this principle to his thought should confirm its general correctness. This is, fortunately, not difficult to do. For example, if one tries to visualize a sentence made up entirely of empty words and syntactical devices, such a congeries of linguistic signs would obviously mean nothing, since they would stand in isolation from the words pointing to the empirical realities of familiar experience. One would in such a case be truly confronted with "air-castles" (G,V,16) or with "a violent divestiture of real objects into naked concepts.... into pure appearances and phenomena." (VII,107). Indeed all of the variegated Hamannian epithets could—certainly with greater justice!—be applied to our congeries of empty words. Surely it was something like this that Hamann had in mind, when he spoke of abstract philosophy as the *"speciosa dehinc miracula* of a deceptive fairy" (VII,108), and when he charged that "this and that philosophy always separates things which cannot be separated at all." For obviously we have here the symbolism of "relations without things."

On the other hand, it is equally plain that a congeries of symbols referring exclusively to empirical realities would also constitute an undecipherable riddle.[38] It is only through the proper union of these two types of symbols that meaning can arise. In the case of a collection of words referring to empirical objects, with all connective words and devices removed, we would have linguistically speaking Hamann's "things without relations."

This duality of linguistic symbolism which we have been describing may be termed "semantic," if that word is understood apart from its connection with contemporary positivistic language philosophies. For it is a duality which is predicated on the basis of meaning. It should be noticed that it is a duality *within* language, and is to be distinguished from the duality of concept and word or of thought and language. As we have seen both dualities are present in Hamann's thought, though confused with one another at crucial points. It is because Unger fails to see this distinction that he is unable to throw any real light on Hamann's language theory, though his treatise on that theory will always remain a valuable guide to certain aspects of Hamann's language philosophy.

Unger charges it against Hamann that "language (in the human sense) is for him at one time an allegory of thoughts, at another, symbolization of external things, again even the reflection of the inner nature of the speaker."[39] But this is precisely the point! If our interpretation is correct, language is for Hamann these three things at once. It is an "allegory of thoughts," in so far as it represents the reflective capacities of the mind. On the other hand, it is a "symbolization of external things," in so far as it reflects the world of empirical objects. This capacity of the mind to symbolize its reflective and perceptive activities at the same time, i.e., of disposing itself toward objects and toward relations simultaneously, implies an "inner nature of the speaker" which transcends its own differentiations, since it is the ground or source of them. Such an explication of Hamann's language philosophy is supported by a typical quotation from Hamann like the following:

> If *sensation* and *understanding*, as the two stems of human knowledge arise from a common, but to us unknown root, so that objects are *given* by means of the former, and *thought* (understood and conceived) by the latter, for what purpose such a violent unwarranted separation of that which nature has joined together? Will not both stems wither and dry up as a result of this dichotomy or schism of their transcendental root? (H.'s italics. VI, 49-50; cf. VII, 10).

It is difficult to see just what this "common, but to us unknown.... transcendental root" may be, if not that which Unger describes as "the inner nature of the speaker" and that which we have described as the capacity of the mind to symbolize both relations and objects, without thereby losing its essential nature, which is the ability to transcend any particular instance of symbolization and to repeat the process indefinitely.

Thus Unger accurately states the meaning of language for Hamann, but he sees in the juxtaposed elements—which his thorough research has led him to find—only contradiction and mutual exclusion. For him, they have no meaning as parts of a larger, more comprehensive whole. But since he consistently interprets Hamann's language philosophy in terms of its alleged Platonism,[40] it is inevitable that he miss the radical nature of the Hamannian ideas. Ironically enough, Hamann, the indefatigable foe of abstraction, produced an idea of language involving a high degree of abstraction, as our study demonstrates. Unger recognizes this, but misses the mark widely, when he characterizes it as "remote from reality."[41] This misunderstanding arises from his inability to see that with Hamann it is not merely the mysterious and remote which must be symbolically represented, but even the familiar data of human experience must likewise be symbolized before there is anything like cognition. (See II,156-157). Symbolism is precisely as necessary for our most immediately given and certain knowledge as for knowledge of the transcendent elements of experience.

The human mind cannot prescribe in advance the proportions of reflective and perceptive symbols in any given statement of natural language. The human being merely speaks meaningfully, and finds that his speech has invariably woven together these two types of symbol, and reflection upon them must always be *a posteriori*. It is undoubtedly the given nature of this symbolic synthesis which caused Hamann to invest it with a religious aura. That he had this synthesis in mind at times appears beyond doubt, although it must be conceded that his statements concerning the unity of language frequently seem to apply specifically to the union of thought and language and not to the union of the discrete elements within language. (Cf. I,449f.) On the other hand, there are utterances which cannot be interpreted on the basis of the unity of thought and language or of concept and word. For example, the description of language as "the finest parable of the hypostatic union of our sensory and rational natures, of the common idiom-exchange of their powers" is meaningless if the thought-language unity is consistently adhered to. For, if the words "sensory and rational natures" are equated with "language and thought respectively—the only logical equivalents in this connection—it would follow that all thought is conceived as "rational," a conception which is manifestly at variance with Hamann's basic doctrines. Moreover, on this interpretation the words "sensory and rational natures" become repetitive of the preceding words "parable" and "hypostatic union." In other words, we are interpreting Hamann as saying that language is "the finest parable of the hypostatic union of language and thought," which is a patent absurdity. In the opinion of this writer, the only meaningful interpretation of this passage is as follows: The perceptive processes of the mind ("sensory nature") and the reflective processes of the mind ("rational nature") function in a living union ("hypostatic union") and are symbolically present in language ("parable") in the form of discrete symbols. In addition to the characterizations of the unity of language which clearly formulate one of the two types of unity under discussion, there are some which may be understood from either standpoint. Such are the descriptions of language as a "shekinah" (VI,34), "tabernacle" (VI,34), "sacrament" (VII, 16), and "koinonía without transubstantiation—neither body nor shadow, but spirit." (VI,170).

It is important to notice the consistently religious terminology which Hamann employs to describe the unity of language. This implies that the idea of the unity of language, however it be conceived, evoked religious feelings in Hamann. Although he does not say so explicitly, we may safely infer that the recognition of the unity of language requires faith. For, if the existence of one's own self and the facts of the external world require faith, even more should the recognition of the given opposites of experience reflected in language require the same. Such faith is essentially a religious faith, since, according to Hamann, the opposites of experience are held together in a living union, not by the power of the human mind, but by the power of God, whose unity "is reflected in the dialect of his works." (II,276).

I do not believe that the attempt to determine as precisely as possible the meaning of the obviously figurative statements concerning the unity of language is misguided. It is conceded that a rigorous analysis of Hamann's statements in general—even where it would seem to be at all possible—would not only be fruitless, but in direct contradiction of his spirit. But it must be remembered that, in spite of its profound religious meaning for Hamann, language constituted for him more nearly a subject of scientific discourse than anything to which he turned his attention, and therefore we may expect him to be logical at this point, if at any.

It may be pointed out that, if the interpretation of his concept of linguistic unity as primarily a unity *within* language be correct, it provides an entirely new criterion by which to judge not only his language theory but virtually all areas of his thought. For, as Cassirer has said, language is the "fixed center" of his philosophy, and the understanding of that center is definitive. Our formulation of Hamann's concept of linguistic unity requires one important step which he did not take—the identification of the relational symbols of ordinary language as the archetypes of abstractions.[42] But since this step seems to be an entirely justified deduction from his general principles, there appears to be no valid reason for not taking the step, especially since it clears up many difficulties.

The puzzling fact is that Hamann himself did not identify the empty words of ordinary language as the archetypes of abstract terms, for not only does such an identification seem immediately implied, but he actually comes close to saying something of this sort on occasion. For instance, he asserts that abstract thought "works over" the "straightforwardness of language" into "pure hieroglyphs and types of ideal relations" or into an "indefinite something$=x$, that nothing remains but the soughing of the wind, a magic phantasmagoria...." But he does not elucidate the notion of the straightforwardness of ordinary language, which he nevertheless says involves our "empirical knowledge." (VII,8). In short, he does not take the final step of identifying the symbols which represent relations in contradistinction to those which represent objects, and find in the former the source of abstractions as relations.[43]

The explanation of this default is beyond question to be found in the fact that the problem of meaning in connection with language philosophy was not discussed in his day.[44] It is an amazing fact that as great a linguist as Otto Jespersen could write as late as 1924 the following line in his *Philosophy of Grammar*: "I may be.... excused if I leave semantics[45] out of consideration in this volume."[46] This scholar considers it sufficient to distinguish between an "inner meaning" and an "outward form" of linguistic phenomena, leaving aside all reference to objective meaning. Thus he holds merely to a word-concept or language-thought duality, which we have already found inadequate for an understanding of Hamann's thought. In the light of the foregoing facts, our surprise at Hamann's failure to formulate a clear statement of the semantic duality in unity of language is somewhat mitigated, and we shall not wonder that Hamann wrote as late as 1784 that "we still lack a *grammar* of reason, as well as of language and its common elements, which are intermingled just as the strings of the psaltery are intertwined, and yet sound harmoniously." (H.'s italics. G,V,22). Until very recent years, the philosophers have sought to consider meaning apart from language, and the grammarians, conversely, have sought to consider language apart from meaning. Obviously this schism of thought and language was unnatural and finally self-stultifying. Here indeed the Hamannian dictum that the philosophers have separated that which nature has joined together may be fittingly invoked. That Hamann could not clarify his own thought on this subject more effectively was due in part to the general state of linguistic philosophy in his day—which was unable to furnish him even with a helpful terminology.

Somewhat earlier we dealt with the concept of the sense-unit, which was defined as the smallest meaningful combination of the linguistic signs of relations and objects. The necessity for the presence of both types of symbols in the sense-unit is now fully apparent. Reality is, according to Hamann's covert doctrine, possessed of a bipolar nature, and therefore every linguistic construction purporting to represent reality must reflect this nature. This is why, on Hamann's interpretation, the conceptual categories of the Aristotelian or Kantian variety are really not the units of thought after all. As abstractions, they represent only one side of reality, namely, relations, and are therefore unipolar. Only in conjunction with truly objective symbolism can they have any meaning. On this view, if the categories of thought are to be determined at all, they must be cast in another form. Their symbolism must conform to the dual or bipolar nature of reality. It is to be noted, however, that this duality is a functional unity. Therefore, one is justified in speaking of the duality in unity of language. Every linguistic unit which manifests this dual nature is likewise possessed of duality in unity.

From the purely philological standpoint, the tacit doctrine of the sense-unit as the irreducible category of language suggests that this is the element common to all languages, however manifold the forms in which it appears. In the first letter of the *Clover Leaf of Hellenic Letters,* Hamann recognizes that all languages have certain "properties" in common. He appeals to what he calls the "migrations of the living languages," whose "mutable pattern" discloses their common elements with the "dead" languages, for light on the problem of the necessary constituents of a universal grammar.[47] "There must be," he stated in the *Essay concerning an Academic Question,* "similarities among all human languages which are based on the uniformity of our nature." (II,121). He does not specify what these "similarities among all human languages" or the "uniformity of our nature" may be, but it may be deduced from his general principles that the similarities among all languages are to be sought in the sense-units, and the uniformity of our nature in the coalescence of the perceptive and reflective powers of the mind as reflected in the sense-unit. Thus indirectly Hamann provides us with his particular answer to the age-old question as to the common elements of all languages. On the basis of this conception it should be possible to predict of a vernacular—in advance of any specific knowledge of it—that it will be possessed of the sense-unit in some form, i.e., of the bipolar symbolism which represents the two aspects of cognition and the two aspects of reality. Therefore, if any sort of apriorism may be properly asserted of Hamann, it must be termed linguistic apriorism. Whether or not the doctrine of the sense-unit is a sound philological principle cannot concern us here. It is interesting to note in passing, however, that our investigation discloses at this point a principle which is capable of empirical verification or refutation, as the case may be.

Confronted as we are with Hamann's implicit doctrine of the indestructible bipolarity of language, we are as near to the foundations of his concept of unity, and therefore of his total philosophy, as it is possible to approach. For here we are face to face with the quintessential symbol of the primordial togetherness, the unity of the created, the mysterious *coincidentia oppositorum* within experience. It is finally this togetherness whose disruption and dissolution Hamann is really decrying, whenever he complains of the scission of natural elements. Linguistic symbolism, properly understood, constitutes the ultimate expression of the "unity of the head as well as the division of the body into its limbs and their *differentia specifica*," which is "the secret of the kingdom of God from its genesis to its apocalypse." (VI,20). Rationalistic philosophy is the persistent attempt to split asunder the unity of the created, to "dissect a body and an event into its first elements," to have relations without things and things without relations. But this attempt—which we shall discuss more thoroughly in the next chapter—must, according to Hamann, fail, for "what God has joined together, no philosophy can put asunder." (G,V,496).

Here, I believe, is the true source of Hamann's long and lasting influence on the poetic creativity of Goethe[48] and the reason for the latter's admission that Hamann was the author from whom he learned most.[49] For Goethe, to whom the "original-phenomenon"[50] (*das Urphänomen*) was indivisible and the occasion for reverential awe, was certainly influenced by no other writer who held to this conception as consistently and as ardently as Hamann. But, with Hamann, the conception is grounded in religious theism in the strictest sense of the word, and, as this study is intended to show, is based on important, if sometimes inarticulate, philosophical insights. Thus, Hamann's conception of the "original-phenomenon" is to be distinguished from Goethe's on two scores: the religious and the philosophical presuppositions. The Magus is often described as a "profound thinker." Nothing justifies this opinion of him more than his implied doctrine of the togetherness of relations and objects and their symbolic distinction within a functional unity. For a concern with terms and their relations is a concern with philosophically basic concepts.

The indissoluble togetherness of the discrete elements of experience, most adequately symbolized in the sense-units of language, is ultimately a creational[51] togetherness. God has joined together from the beginning what reason attempts to separate. With this principle in mind, we cannot be surprised at Hamann's vigorous opposition to any theory of the human origin of language. It was inevitable that Herder's anthropocentric theory of the origin of language should elicit Hamann's animadversions.

The problem of the origin of language was much discussed during the period of the Enlightenment. But Hamann's views on the subject were not formulated until the appearance of Herder's prize-winning essay, *Treatise on the Origin of Language* (1772). Herder's principal argument is that man, in contrast to animals, possesses the capacity of reflection (*Besonnenheit*). Reflection enables him to single out one wave from the ocean of sensations which flood in upon him, and to preserve that one wave as a characteristic feature (*Merkmal*) of the experience which produced it. Thus the bleating of the lamb suggests itself as the characteristic feature or *Merkmal* of that animal. Herder held that animals have a language, but not in the sense of human language. Man's inferiority to the animals in strength and instinct is compensated by his far greater mental faculties, which differ from those of the animals not merely in degree, but also in kind.[52]

Herder's theory makes room for the argument that man invented language (Bacon, Locke) as well as for the opposed doctrine that language arose from the sounds of nature (Condillac), and herein no doubt lay its great appeal to his contemporaries. But Herder's argument virtually eliminates the necessity for the creative activity of God. It is this aspect of his theory which evoked Hamann's censure. Hamann did not take up a position like that of Süssmilch, who conceived of God as intervening to solve an otherwise insoluble enigma. Hamann countered Herder's arguments by undertaking to demonstrate the latter's inconsistencies and by appealing to general principles.[53]

Hamann found Herder's theory of the origin of language unacceptable on two scores. First, it credits man rather than God with the creation of language. Secondly, it oversimplifies the facts of the linguistic process. Instead of recognizing that everything within experience is divine and human at the same time, Herder fell into the old error of the rationalists, and attempted to understand man apart from God. "But everything divine is also human," Hamann wrote in *The Last Will and Testament of the Knight of Rosenkreuz concerning the Divine and Human Origin of Language* in answer to Herder. (IV,23). "This *communicatio* of divine and human *idiomatum* is a fundamental law and the main key of all our knowledge and of the entire visible economy (*Haushaltung*)." (IV,24). In Hamann's judgment, Herder sought to render human reason independent of God and to absolutize its power. Hence stems his demurrer and his irony with regard to Herder's theory.

Since everything is at once divine and human, it follows that language arose from the co-activity of God and man. (IV,24). The duality in unity of natural language is a symbol of the duality in unity of its origin, of the *communicatio idiomatum* of the human and divine. In crediting reflection (*Besonnenheit*) with creative power, Herder was, in effect, ignoring the dual nature of mind.[54] In the light of our previous interpretation, the following formulation of Hamann's criticism of Herder seems to follow. Since all cognition is dependent upon some kind of verbalization, according to Herder's view, abstract language had to precede natural language. For reflection apart from perception can only produce abstract language. But it cannot be true that abstract language is prior in time to natural language. Hence, Herder's theory of the human origin of language is false. But, since it renders superfluous the creational togetherness of the discrete elements of mind and experience, it is not only false: it is irreligious. It is destructive of the "sacramental" nature of language, a nature imparted to language by the Creator.

By way of recapitulation of the argument of this chapter, we may say that language seems to be naturally the bearer of two distinguishable types of symbols, which are best differentiated on the basis of relations and objects or on the basis of the reflective and perceptive capacities of the mind. Natural language is veridical in nature, because it deals in real relations and real objects. The purely relational symbolism of ordinary or natural language is susceptible, however, of expansion into abstractions. How this occurs, Hamann's thought gives us no clue, but we do know that he considered abstract terms as indicating "mere relations." These terms must, in turn, be used in conjunction with the normal relational symbolism of ordinary language so that entire sentences in the abstract form are seen to be exclusively relational in reference. The dual or bipolar nature of language in the natural state has therefore been cancelled, and such transformed language is held to be merely unipolar in reference. In other words, the duality in unity of natural language has been destroyed. Objectively considered, this represents a divorce of language from one aspect of external experience; subjectively considered, it represents a hypertrophy of the reflective capacities of the mind and an atrophy of the perceptive capacities.

It was further found that, although Hamann did not break with the traditional grammatical notion of parts of speech, isolated words cannot, on his principles, be the units of language, since linguistic symbolism must always manifest a dual nature. That is, every genuine unit of language must be possessed of the distinct symbolism of relations and objects or of reflection and perception. The inevitable togetherness of these discrete elements is due to the creative act of God, and represents the most important unity within cognitive experience, since it is, in the words of Hugo Delff,a "visible image"[55] of the interaction of the ideal and real.

## CHAPTER IV

### REASON AND EXPERIENCE

If, as Hamann maintains, the final aim of the rationalist is to render man completely independent of objective experience, i.e., to break through "the confines of sensory experience"[1] to an absolutely autonomous position, he must entirely eliminate language. For linguistic symbols, whether abstract or not, "belong with their elements to *sensation and intuition.*" (H.'s italics. VII,13). Although he cannot accomplish this end, it is possible for the rationalist, with the aid of the "most powerful acid of reason" (IV,436), to destroy the bipolar nature of language. In other words, since he cannot destroy the basic union of language and thought, he compromises by destroying the union of language with experience. Since language represents the final and most important link with experience, it is possible according to Hamann to understand the schismatic effect of rationalism upon the union of reason and experience by a consideration of the effects of excessive ratiocination upon language.

The rationalist shares with the mystic a dissatisfaction with natural language, but unlike the mystic he does not seek to dispense with language entirely in order to gain an immediate insight into the nature of reality. The rationalistic procedure involves reducing language to "empty" or relational symbolism, which is adequate for the space and time categories of the mathematical disciplines, but which is totally inadequate for interpreting the meaning of life. The unquestionable successes of a Galileo, Kepler, and Newton as pure scientists cannot establish them or their methods as authoritative in the fields of philosophy and religion. (IV,25; cf. VI,39). The mathematical spirit in philosophy and religion, though its ideal aim is to eliminate that residuum of experience found in language, contents itself with its partial rejection of language. In the following paragraphs we shall note Hamann's estimate of the abstract method in general and then his reckoning with the thought of two contemporary thinkers of the first rank.

In the otherwise inept characterization of the Magus' life and thought in the *Encyclopaedia Britannica* the author makes one statement which comes very near to the truth about Hamann: "His fundamental thought is the unsatisfactoriness of abstraction."[2] Now, although this statement omits all reference to Hamann's constructive views, it is, with certain provisions, an adequate formulation of the negative aspects of his thought. For this is the ever reiterated refrain of his "authorship" with regard to the great architectonic philosophic systems, and it is expressed with all the cogency, wit, satire, and even abuse that he can command. His valid insights into the nature of the abstracting process have been inadequately treated even by sympathetic scholars largely because of his all too often vituperative approach to the subject.

The following statements and characterizations of abstractions will serve to give the reader a general idea of the Hamannian opinion and feeling in this connection. It should be said, however, that here, as almost everywhere else, it is exceedingly difficult, if not impossible, to give an adequate English rendering of his terminology. "A general term," he wrote, "is an empty bag (*leerer S|chlauch*), which changes its shape every moment, and, overextended, bursts." (G,V,513). Such descriptions as the following are applied to abstract language: "fancies" (*Hirngespinnste*) (G,V, 516); "wax noses," i.e., deceivers (VII,420); "the handiwork of sophistry" (VII,420); even "thief and murderer." (VII,36). The fancies of reason are used in the "arbitrary construction of philosophical primers and Bibles." (G,V,517). The arch-abstraction is, however, the term "reason" itself. "What," he asked rhetorically, "is most blessed *reason* with its universality, infallibility, extravagance, certainty, and evidence?" Thereupon he answered his own question: "An *ens rationis*, a dumb idol, to which a *noisy* superstition of unreason ascribes *divine attributes*." (H.'s italics. VI,16). Sometimes reason and its products appear as passive creatures of the mind;[3] at other times they appear as active and even vicious enemies of the truth.[4] This imputation of a twofold nature to abstractions is illuminating for Hamann's critique of reason and language. "A small addition of new concepts has invariably changed the language of philosophy" (I,388), and this transmuted language has itself become a fruitful source of error.

Not only are individual words of this type subjective, but, according to Hamann, entire systems constructed by means of them are mere displays of subjectivity with no genuine conformity to the structure of reality. As he opined of the Kantian *Critique*: "Nothing but pure words, pure concepts, for which the thing exists nowhere, nor can be proved." (G,V,518). In discussing the philosophers Spinoza and Franz Hemsterhuis (1720-1790), Hamann wrote that the "Euclidian shell of the one and Platonic shell of the other" were both "untrustworthy" as far as he was concerned. (G,V,603). Yet there are undoubtedly some things in Spinoza which Hamann, despite basic differences between the men, should have and under more favorable circumstances no doubt would have appreciated.[5] This we may conclude from his attitude toward Rousseau, the content of whose religious philosophy is actually alien to Hamann's historically and Biblically oriented views, but who never elicited the animadversions which Spinoza did. The uncongenial ideas of Spinoza's philosophy were rendered for Hamann all the more distasteful by the former's method. Since the German word for spider is *Spinne*, Hamann exploited the similarity in form to the name Spinoza, and compared the Dutch philosopher's system to *Spinneweben* or spiderwebs. (I,438). In this vein, he wrote: "The geometrical structure is natural for spiders and their admirer, Spinoza." (III,192). Carrying out the analogy further, he remarked, with scarcely pardonable irony, that Spinoza's method can catch only small insects. Franz Hemsterhuis, likewise, though he manifests many affinities with Hamann,[6] affronted the latter with the form of his philosophy, the "Platonic shell." Hamann conceded that the Platonic method may have been useful against the Sophists, but he saw it as finally unacceptable. Thus, his generally high estimate of Plato did not extend to the latter's method, to which he applied the epithet "mousetrap." (G,V,636).

In the Platonic and Euclidian-Spinozistic methods Hamann saw simply the relational symbolism of language transformed into qualitative symbolism and finally hypostatized as real entities. The analogy between such philosophizing and the activity of spiders and silkworms is, for his purposes, quite apt, for he judged that thinkers employing such methods are engaged in spinning systems out of their own resources very much as these creatures spin their respective webs and cocoons out of their own bodies. (III,192). Therefore, such systems are visible displays of the imbalance of language, for the subjective element has completely eliminated the objective element.

In Hamann's rejection of the scholastic method we encounter a genuinely Lutheran motif. For he shares with the great reformer a distrust of discursive reasoning in theology. Luther's judgment that "only without Aristotle can we become theologians"[7] can be adopted as descriptive of Hamann's opinion, if the name "Aristotle" is understood as a symbol of the scholastic method in general. His rejection of this method, like Luther's, was carried out in the interest of a Biblically oriented theology. "Reason and Scripture," he wrote to Jacobi, "are basically the same thing: the language of God." (G,V,247).

The use of the abstract method, however, constitutes an implied rejection of experience. The deep-seated aversion to experience which characterizes the rationalist is best revealed in his struggle to free himself from the language of God and the language of man, thus from religious experience and all external experience whatsoever. Let us now consider the struggle of the rationalist to declare himself independent of experience in so far as that struggle is exemplified by two great contemporaries of Hamann.

Blanke remarks in his essay "Hamann and Lessing" that "Johann Georg Hamann, the brilliant witness to the gospel in the period of the Enlightenment, found in his age only two opponents who were worthy of him: Lessing and Kant."[8] Hamann's indictment of these two men was that they attempted to nullify the natural bond of man with experience. It is immaterial that Lessing was attempting to separate man from the Biblical revelation, and that Kant was attempting to separate man from ordinary human speech. Both were engaged in fundamentally the same task—to render reason autonomous. Both men criticized the claims made on behalf of reason by the typical Enlighteners, but according to Hamann they were nevertheless both infected with the same faith in reason. It is in his judgment of Lessing's view of revelation that Hamann's theological differences with the Enlightenment are brought into sharpest focus.

With regard to revelation Lessing's thesis may be thus summarized:[9] Individual experience of Christ as a present reality is necessary to establish his divinity. But it is impossible to establish that divinity on the basis of miracles, since the miracles recorded deal with past events. As past realities they cannot convince in the present. That which can convince in the present, however, is Christ's doctrines, for they manifest an inner logic which commends them to us as necessary rational truths. But once apprehended through the medium of the historical revelation, the revelatory record may then fall away. Thus the revelatory form is accidental. Obviously the virtual autonomy of reason is guaranteed, for revelation is simply a medium through which reason is brought to a consciousness of its own powers.[10]

Lessing's estimate of revelation differed from that of the orthodox Enlighteners in that, whereas they desired an immediate break with the necessity for revelation, and desired at once to supplant faith with reason and revealed religion with natural religion, Lessing considered it necessary to delay the severance from the Biblical record until such time when mankind shall have attained the age of maturity. At some future stage in the development of mankind, revelation, by virtue of the augmented rationality of mankind, may be dispensed with. This naturally follows from his principles as explicated in the *Education of the Human Race* that humanity, conceived as a sort of corporate individual, is in process of education from a less rational to a more rational mode of existence. On Lessing's view, Hamann charged, God must be conceived as a *summus paedogogus* who is gradually guiding his pupil, the human race, to be less and less dependent upon revelational experience and to become more and more dependent upon reason. (VI,128). Or, to state it another way, God is engaged in guiding mankind out of the age of faith into the age of reason. This process constitutes, in effect, a transition from a state of heteronomy to a state of autonomy. In contrast with the other Enlighteners, who conceived God as a *summus philosophus* (VI,128), and who were willing to engage confidently even in the present age in a search for eternal truths to supersede the truths of revelation, Lessing was merely inclined to postpone the ideal of autonomous reason until a future stage be reached. Hamann's opinion of Lessing's theology may be summed up in his own words from a letter to Herder in 1780 concerning the *Education of the Human Race*, which had just appeared: "Nothing but the transmigration of ideas into new formulas and words. . . . no reformation-spirit, no conception which might deserve a Magnificat."[11]

This reckoning of Hamann with Lessing is exceedingly important not only for an understanding of the former, but also for an understanding of the intellectual history of eighteenth century Germany, for we have here a settling of accounts between two critics of the Enlightenment who had otherwise a great deal in common. Both were enemies of the Wolffian rationalism in *belles lettres*[12] and in religion.[13] Both appealed to Luther as their mentor.[14] Both were bearers of the critical spirit of the Enlightenment, a spirit which was willing, if necessary, to turn even upon itself. And yet it is patent that a great gulf separated them, a gulf which Hamann clearly recognized. This gulf was constituted by Lessing's virtual rejection of experience, a rejection which may be made clearer by his implied endorsement of a type of rational proposition contingently available for religious knowledge.[15]

An analysis of Lessing's idea of the gradual emancipation of reason from revelation by virtue of the self-authenticating nature of Christ's teachings reveals that he was simply withdrawing temporarily from a more to a less ambitious estimate of rationalism. If the essence of the Leibniz-Wolffian rationalism required in the last resort an appeal to the analytic judgment,[16] i.e., to the type of proposition in which the predicate is obtained by analysing the subject, then Lessing may be said, in effect, to have rejected contingently this type of judgment in his view of revelation. Although in his writings on religion Lessing was dealing primarily with what would have later been called value-judgments, we may simply treat them as factual judgments for the purpose of clarification. In admitting the necessity of the "historical truths" of revelation for an initial insight into their validity, he was at the same time conceding that the answer was not known beforehand, i.e., the predicate was not really contained in the subject. However, after revelation has made clear the nature of the subject—here Christ's doctrines—reason could thereupon confirm their truth, and thereafter deduce all that is further necessary. By way of parallel, it might be suggested that Lessing was here adopting for his view of revelation something very much like Kant's synthetic judgment *a priori*, since he admitted the original necessity of experience. But the parallel ends here, for Lessing apparently looked for the day when something like the analytic judgment would be restored, i.e., when reason should have become sufficiently rational to dispense even with the initial necessity for revelation,[17] whereas Kant never looked for the day when the human mind should have so developed that experience would no longer be necessary for the synthetic judgment *a priori*.

But even though experience in the form of Biblical revelation was still required by Lessing for the first flash of insight into the truth of Christ's teachings, it virtually guaranteed in Hamann's eyes the autonomy of reason. For here there is no necessity for constant recourse to experience, in this case to revelation.[18] One can imagine the effect of this proposition on the Magus, for whom the "repeated reading" (I,53) of the Scriptures was a confirmed habit, and who not only "dared to make the Bible the starting point of his thinking,"[19] but who made it the constant and final norm of his entire philosophy. In the end, he saw no more real difference between Lessing's and Wolff's theology than between what he ironically termed "the powerful differences of analytic and synthetic judgments." (VII,4; cf. VI, 49). Both establish the virtual apriority of religious knowledge.

Another point to be noticed in Lessing's thought is the discontinuity between reason and the temporal-historical process. He asserts that "accidental historical truth can never become proof of the necessary truths of reason."[20] That is to say, there are two kinds of religious truth, one merely historical, the other purely rational. The implication is that rational truth is superior to historical truth, or, to state it still another way, truth manifested in the temporal process is discontinuous with rational truth. This constitutes, according to Lessing, "the loathsome, wide ditch across which I cannot get, however often and earnestly I have attempted the leap."[21] This is virtually a declaration of reason's independence of the time-process in so far as it is history. But for Hamann historical truths were both "temporal and eternal" at once (VII,57); the two cannot be separated and set over against one another. For reason itself is a fragment of history,[22] and the truths which it apprehends are no "eternal truths" alone, but are also "constantly temporal" truths. (VII,41). Thus, for him there can be no double religious truth, with one aspect taking precedence over the other.

Although Lessing's theory of revelation elicited from the Magus a criticism which is most enlightening with reference to the latter's thought-world, no account of the generally schismatic effect of reason upon the togetherness of reason and experience is complete apart from reference to Kant. Not only was Hamann the personal friend of Kant—though in a peculiar and limited sense—for more than a quarter of a century, but he was also always the interested spectator and remarkable critic of Kant's achievements. The relationship of the Magus to Kant is a long and interesting story,[23] and it is reflected in epic proportions in letters like that of the twenty-fifth of July, 1759 to Kant and in writings like the *Socratic Memoirs* (1759) and the *Metacritique* (1784). Kant's effort, at the instance of a mutual friend, J. C. Berens, to dissuade the young Hamann from the religious standpoint he had adopted after his religious experience of 1758,[24] his overture to Hamann for the purpose of securing the latter as a collaborator on a proposed textbook in physics for children,[25] and his assistance in Hamann's procurement of a minor position with the tax authorities of East Prussia in 1767 provide valuable material for the interpretation of each of these men individually and in their interrelationship. It is, however, preëminently in Hamann's response to the *Critique of Pure Reason* that one finds the fundamental differences between the thought of the two men laid bare.

One of the most striking things about the Hamannian estimate of Kant is the revaluation which it has undergone in recent years. Time was when it was simply taken for granted in scholarly circles—even if with an ineffectual dissent here and there[26]—that Hamann totally failed to understand Kant, and the former's metacritical work was therefore dismissed as an "experience of misunderstanding."[27] But with regard to this opinion various commentators have, especially in the last quarter of a century, vigorously demurred, adducing solid reasons for so doing. Thus, Blanke,[28] Nadler,[29] and Metzke,[30] approaching Hamann from the theological, literary, and philosophical standpoints respectively, and with over a century and a half of scholarly investigation of the Hamannian problem behind them, concur in the opinion that Hamann not only understood the Kantian philosophy, but that what he had to say concerning it is significant indeed. The increasing dissatisfaction with the stereotyped misinterpretation of Hamann's philosophic efforts and the need for an objective revaluation moved the *Königsberger Gelehrte Gesellschaft* about two decades ago to offer a prize for the best essay on Hamann's philosophy.[31] If it be true that the comprehension of Hamann's meaning has grown with the years, events have proved Goethe wrong in his prediction that Hamann's writings would become more and more incomprehensible to future generations.[32] It is true that Hamann's allusions are obscurer to the twentieth century than to the eighteenth; but it is equally true that the twentieth century is more receptive to his basic ideas than the eighteenth. After all, Hamann himself looked for an increasing understanding of his purpose and his major ideas with the passage of time. "One easily overcomes the double affliction," he wrote in *The Crusades of the Philologist,* "of not being *understood* by his contemporaries, and therefore of being *mistreated,* through the *taste* of the *abilities* of a better *posterity.*" (H.'s italics. II,114).

Those who charge Hamann with failure to understand the philosophical systems he attacked are right in one respect and quite wrong in another and more important respect. They are right, in so far as they mean by "understanding" a thorough exploration of the details of a system after the manner of an auditor examining financial records for calculational errors. They are wrong, however, in so far as they mean by that term a grasp of the fundamental presuppositions of a philosophy, its general method, and its immediate and ultimate consequences. A few months before his death, Hamann wrote: "I still consider it fruitless labor to do patchwork on subordinate principles and to discover their contradiction." (G,V,637). It is an error to suppose that Hamann's opposition to abstract thinking arose from intellectual incapacity. It may be true, as Bertrand Russell asserts, that "many people have a passionate hatred of abstraction. . . . because of its intellectual difficulty; but as they do not wish to give this reason, they invent all sorts of others that sound grand."[33] But to this class of persons Hamann does not belong. Even his most merciless critics have conceded his ability, though deploring at the same time his antirationalistic tendencies.[34] Actually Hamann utilized abstraction in his campaign against abstraction. Therefore, Unger was led to complain of the abstractness of Hamann's central notion of language.[35] As this study is designed to show, there is inescapably implied in the Hamannian language philosophy a trenchant criticism of the abstracting process, and indeed what is explicit is a very instructive and valuable criticism. Hamann perceived deeply and wrestled constantly with the problem summed up by Whitehead in his statement that "thought is abstract; and the intolerant use of abstractions is the major vice of the intellect."[36] Having cleared the ground for Hamann's reckoning with the critical philosophy of Kant, we may now proceed to examine that reckoning in its essential features.

On the basis of the Magus' presuppositions, it is not difficult to understand why he condemned the great speculative systems of philosophy. Yet, one should expect from him a feeling of sympathy and appreciation for the efforts of his compatriot, Kant. For it was the latter's self-imposed task to define the limits of reason. ". . . . It is my task to answer the question," he wrote, "how far reason can go, without the material presented and the aid furnished by experience."[37] If the Enlighteners had promised all things in the name of reason, Kant attempted to show what could be legitimately expected of it. If, from our point of historical vantage, we are able to see Kant's work clearly as one of the great water-sheds in the history of intellectual development, it was not so easy for his contemporaries to appraise his significance for the future.[38] Mendelssohn, who distinguished himself from most of the contemporary rationalists by his clairvoyance as to Kant's radical significance, if not with reference to his grasp of Kant's system, symbolized for all the orthodox Enlighteners the actual state of affairs. He accepted stoically the dashing of his philosophic hopes by the "all-destroying Kant."[39] "I know," he confessed by way of capitulation, "that my philosophy is no longer the philosophy of the times."[40] On the other hand, there were those who sensed in Kant a danger from another side, and, to use Höffding's phrase, afforded "significant opposition."[41] Chief among these was Hamann, who was joined by Herder and Jacobi. It was the non-rational aspects of human nature and traditional values which they saw threatened by the Kantian critique, and which they were determined should not be minimized or ignored.

As far as Hamann was concerned, Kant's modified rationalism was, if anything, more dangerous than the vulnerable rationalism of Wolff; for Hamann, it meant simply the strategic retreat of rationalism to an allegedly impregnable citadel. Though Hamann was one of the very first to publish his reactions to the *Critique*, the form his answer was to take required time for its development. A few months after the appearance of the *Critique*, however, he compared Kant favorably with Hume—a compliment to Kant—but he qualified this by asserting that he preferred Hume, since the latter recognized the rôle of faith in knowledge. (VI, 187). However much Hamann should have had in common with Kant, in the end he repudiated and reprobated Kantianism. We saw that Lessing was for the Magus always at heart an Enlightener; so likewise was Kant. As Metzke says:

> It is necessary to see this reckoning of Hamann with Kant in relation to Hamann's general attack on the Enlightenment. Only thus—and not in isolation—will one understand it properly, and—without apology!—do justice to it, for thus Hamann saw Kant. Everything that Hamann wrote to Kant or against Kant is, in principle, a reckoning with the Enlightenment.[42]

Hamann's evaluation of the *Critique* is found chiefly in his *Review of the Critique of Pure Reason*, in the *Metacritique*, and in his letters. I shall draw chiefly on the *Metacritique* as containing the essence of his criticism. The question has always been raised as to whether this essay really concerns itself with Kant's system at all. This question may be answered affirmatively or negatively, according to the point of view. It is plain that Hamann does not criticize Kant on the latter's own terms. He could not agree that reason can be its own arbiter, its own "organon and criterion." Therefore, he could not embark upon a detailed criticism. Rather he preferred to "keep to the foundation-pillars, which are worm-eaten." (VII,315). The foundation pillars are constituted by logic in divorce from experience. Kant had clearly laid it down that it was his aim to trade the limits of reason by means of reason itself. "Common logic," he wrote, "presents me with a complete and systematic catalogue of all the simple operations of reason."[43] But for Hamann the only arbiter of reason was language. As we saw in the previous chapter, reason and experience become cognitively effective in language only, where their characteristic symbols are distinguishable from one another. Therefore it is unwarranted to abstract a part and to set the part up as the organon of the whole.[44]

If the objection be raised at this juncture that Hamann himself had recourse to logic in his attempt to refute Kant, and therefore vitiated somewhat his own argument, it must be conceded that this is the case, but the important fact for our understanding of him is that in the process he called attention to the empirical fact of language as the *sine qua non* of rational discourse, a fact which in Hamann's view Kant ignored. Hamann's struggle here was to find a common universe of discourse with Kant. It is idle to consider the self-consistency of another's discourse, if one does not wish to discourse at all about that subject. If Kant's *Critique* may be described as an investigation of reason in the light of reason, the *Metacritique* may be described as a prolegomenon to an investigation of reason in the light of language.

The *Metacritique* provides us with what might be called, in Spenglerian terms, a morphology of the history of the rational method in philosophy. Hamann desired to set the Kantian effort to delimit the province of reason in its world-historical framework. According to Hamann, it is the second great stage in the evolution, or better, devolution of reason. The first stage was attained in the Enlightenment, when reason was freed from dependence upon social experience, i.e., tradition. "The first purification of philosophy consisted in the partly misunderstand, partly unsuccessful attempt to make reason independent of all custom and tradition and all faith in them." (VII,5). Here Hamann had reference to the attempts of the pre-Kantian rationalists to free reason of all heteronomous influences—the authoritative church, the authoritative book or creed, and the authoritative political system. In this stage, reason asserted an autonomous character, as opposed to its former heteronomous character. Formerly it was in the service of tradition; now it attacked and disposed of tradition. Lessing, though he provisionally retained the Biblical revelation must, as we have seen, be included here. The second stage in the "purification" of reason was reached in the work of Kant. For it was he who attempted to divorce reason from the one thing the Enlighteners had left in company with it, namely, individual experience. "The second purification," Hamann continued, "is even more transcendental and aims at freedom from experience and its everyday induction." (VII,5). This constitutes Kant's contribution, his "purism." But even at this stage there still remains an empirical element—language. For the visible and audible signs of language belong to experience. Yet it is precisely from experience that Kant seeks to separate reason, in order to establish its just claims.

But Kant does not lead us into the third and final stage of the process of purification. By way of irony, Hamann suggests the development of the last stage of reason, the stage of complete autonomy. "The third, highest and, as it were, empirical purism concerns therefore language, the first and last organon and criterion of reason, without any other credentials than tradition and usage." (VII,6). This is further, however, than Kant can go, for it is manifestly impossible to separate the invisible meaning or conceptual correlate entirely from its empirical form in what Hamann termed the "sacrament of language." (VII,16). Kant still must depend on his rarefied abstract terminology. As a result the third purism must necessarily suffer shipwreck. But the advantage of this *reductio ad absurdum* is that it reveals the fundamental error in the whole process of purification. The error consists in attempting to separate that which cannot be separated. "Sensation and understanding" have "a common root" which nourishes both as long as they remain in living contact with it (VII,10), i.e., as long as they remain united in the manner in which natural language unites them.

It may further be noted that Kant is charged with an "old cold prejudice in favor of mathematics."[45] This is held to account for his apriorism, and is the logical outcome of his "gnostic hatred for matter" or "mystical love for form." (VII,7). Thus the progress of reason on its journey of purification is not a progress into life, but an egress from life, or from sense experience.

A word should be said here about the charge that Kant was motivated by a "mystical love for form." For one of the most fundamental characteristics of Hamann also is his devotion to form. Indeed, in an important sense all of his writings subsequent to his conversion were designed to constitute an apology for the form of revelation as ultimately inseparable from its content. But it should be noticed that he indicted Kant for his "mystical love for form." By this Hamann apparently meant a love for form conceived as interior to the mind, i.e., for the mathematically ideal form. Since it was Hamann's concern to call attention to the union of inner and outer experience in the "sacrament of language," Kant's attempt to separate the two could only appear to him strange indeed. That Kant attempted to execute a thorough critical investigation upon the differentia of reason and experience by virtually ignoring the most important form of experience, namely, language, was incomprehensible to the man who described his philosophy as "verbalism." But Kant did not, for he could not, carry his thought to its logical conclusion. He did not enter upon the third stage of purification, which Hamann maintained to be the inevitable culmination of this tendency. Thus Kant does not really belong to those who openly abjure the word. He was too much of the reformer of language—even though unwittingly—for that. Therefore, in the end Hamann's ascription of mystical tendencies to Kant must be interpreted as an admonition to that thinker.

If we translate Hamann's thought as outlined in the preceding paragraphs into the terms I have suggested as being helpful in the interpretation of his philosophy, we arrive at something like this: By virtue of their greater confidence in reason, the Enlighteners expanded the symbolism of relations— which is found in natural language in the form of syntactical or "empty" words and devices—into abstractions, and thereupon proceeded to regard these abstractions as faithful surrogates for real entities, from which might be deduced a great deal of knowledge of a theological, cosmological, and generally ontological character.

Kant, however, dissatisfied with the extravagant claims of the Enlighteners, confined himself, as it were, to that which is verbally represented in natural language by the empty words and syntactical devices mentioned above, and found that they tell us precisely nothing except the relations of space and time, either grammatically or philosophically speaking.[46] But since they do tell us this much, he posited time and space as pure forms of intuition. For, in the words of the *Critique of Pure Reason,* "the transcendental Aesthetic cannot contain any more than these two elements—space and time."[47] Of course, Kant was unaware of his debt to language in this procedure, and since he failed to recognized that debt, it is not surprising that he arrived at the notion that space and time are subjective. That is, if he overlooked his obvious debt to language, it was inevitable that he also overlook his less obvious debt to experience for the concepts of space and time. Kant was willing, within limits, to expand the relational symbolism of natural language into qualities, hence into abstractions, but was careful to avoid the error of the earlier rationalists and refused to assign an ontological status to them. His modesty in this regard, however, does not compensate for his failure to recognize that there can be no "pure," i.e., experience-free forms of intuition. Hence, the final stage of the purification of reason can never be reached, and the most ambitious attempt of all to establish the independence of reason has suffered shipwreck.

The preceding paragraphs are, of course, a hypothetical statement of what seems implied in Hamann's critique of Kantianism in the light of our interpretation of his language theory. Not only does such an interpretation seem to follow from his major premises but also it does not conflict with his characteristic conclusions concerning the nature of language. In his own way, Hamann was addressing himself to the same problem as Kant—the problem as to what is presupposed in the cognitive process. Here follows the general answer to that question:

> If it therefore still remains a principal question as to *how the capacity to think is possible*—the capacity to think, *to the right of* and *to the left of, before* and *without, with* and *beyond* experience, no deduction is necessary to establish the genealogical priority of *language* and its heraldry over the seven sacred functions of logical propositions and conclusions. Not only the entire capacity to think rests on language .... but language is also *the center of the misunderstanding of reason with itself.* .... (H.'s italics VII, 9).

We have already considered the process by which language becomes "the center of the misunderstanding of reason with itself."

Kant constructed, Hamann says, "the magic castle of his critique" by means of language, and by means of a proper understanding of language "can the structure be dissolved."[48]

> With me the question is not so much: What is reason? but rather: What is language? and here I presume to be the basis of all paralogisms and antinomies which one blames on the former; therefore it happens that one takes words for concepts and concepts for the things themselves. (G, V, 15).

Thus the paralogisms and antinomies, which play such an important part in Kant's philosophy, are held to be traceable to language, and not to reason.[49]

Hamann concluded the *Metacritique* with the statement that he left it to each reader "to unfold the clenched fist into an open hand." (VII,16). Our attempt to do this has consisted in the linking of abstractions, as the signs of relations, with the "empty" words of ordinary discourse, and, in the light of this identification, we have undertaken a reconsideration of his verbalistic philosophy. If this interpretation seems to give a somewhat positivistic coloring to his theory of language, I nevertheless believe that it is quite in his in this area. But this tendency must be set over against his religious beliefs, particularly over against his belief in a transcendent God. In Hamann there is a singular witness to the upward sweep of revelation toward heavenly things and simultaneously to the downward sweep of that same revelation toward earthly things. On the one hand, he could assert that "our philosophy must begin from heaven and not from the *theater anatomicum* and the dissection of a cadaver" (VII,149), and, on the other hand, that his philosophy "stands and walks with its feet on the ground." (VII,400). Blanke recognizes the importance of this facet of Hamann's thought, and stresses what he terms the principle of *Geistleiblichkeit* as one of Hamann's four basic theological principles.[50] In the *Metacritique* Hamann charges that Kant violates this principle by "separating things which cannot be separated at all."

Whatever may be the final judgment of scholarship upon Hamann's metacritical work, there can be no doubt that we do find in it most valuable insights into the Hamannian thought-world and a valid criticism of Kant for his neglect of the relation of language to cognition. With reference to this latter point we find

Hamann anticipating modern developments in philosophy. It is indeed astonishing to find him emphasizing in the latter half of the eighteenth century the centrality of language in all thought.[51] It is true that he did not think his principles through to their logical conclusion, but it must be remembered that others did not travel as far as he did along this road. When he wrote to Jacobi in 1787 the line: "What in your language is 'being' I should prefer to call the 'word'," he was speaking not only to Jacobi but to the whole company of those whose discourse was in terms of the traditional philosophy of Western culture. Hamann would have had to be born in the twentieth century for that statement to meet with serious consideration. Therefore, that he accomplished as much as he did despite his isolation in this area and despite his own personal shortcomings is impressive. At the least, one must concur in Hegel's opinion that in the *Metacritique*—the concentrated essence of the Hamannian verbalistic philosophy—we have to do with a "remarkable" and "ingenious" essay.[52]

Hamann felt that those who sit confidently in judgment on the final questions of human existence, relying principally upon reason, can usually be shown to be blind or naive with reference to experience close at hand or, as he put it, "befuddled in their domestic affairs." (IV,25). His favorite and most important example of this was, of course, the myopia of the rationalists with reference to language. Lessing exemplifies the violence done upon the divine word by autonomous reason; Kant exemplifies the violence done upon the human word by that same reason. Thus it is the perennial tendency of reason to attempt the withdrawal from language and therefore from experience. But since the rationalist will speak, he must have recourse to language, even if rationally transformed language. But his discourse is in as it were purely syntactical symbols. The bipolar unity of language has been destroyed by excessive reflection.

The uniting bond of reason and experience, "the bond of nature" (G,V,517), which is rendered visible or audible by the duality in unity of natural language, is exterior to the mind, indeed it lies in the bosom of ultimate reality. Its character is secret and hidden,[53] and is a mystery of the creation. Kant's assertion that the union of reason and experience is effected by the mind by virtue of his doctrine that the categories of understanding and intuition are united by means of the productive imagination[54] Hamann could not accept. (VII,6). He could not accept it any more than one could accept the proposition that the mind can prescribe in advance the proportions of relational and objective symbolism in any given statement of ordinary language. First, the statement must be made, and then one is in a position to compare the two types of symbols. Obviously something other than imagination has been the determining factor in their union, for in order to be accepted as true, the statement must correspond to reality, and reality is not interior to the mind. The Kantian device of the productive imagination could be for Hamann but another means whereby Kant desired to render the mind independent of experience, for in this case the uniting bond in a product of the mind, even if "concealed in the depths of the soul."

Only on the basis of Hamann's view of the decisive importance of natural language for cognition do his ambitious claims for a verbalistic philosophy make sense. Consider the following lines, written to Jacobi about a year before his death, when he should have been a broken and beaten man on account of his ill health, his poverty, and his vocational crises:

> Idealism and realism—Christianity and Lutheranism. The former two are in my eyes ideal—the latter two real. Between your two extremes there is lacking a mean, which I might call verbalism. My twins are not extremes, but allies and closely related. I desire to refute the *Berlin* idealization of Christianity and Lutheranism by means of a historical and physical realism, to oppose *experience to pure reason*. To straighten out this tangle is precisely the herculean task which I have in mind, because I do not know at which end I should properly attack the matter. As you yourself say, the real remains, the ideal depends more on us, and is mutable by means of nominalism. Our concepts of things are mutable by means of a new language, by means of new signs, which make us aware of new relations or rather restore the oldest, original, true ones.
>
> . . . . . . . . . . .
>
> Christianity and Lutheranism are *res facti*, living organs and instruments of the Godhead and humanity.[55]

It should be remembered that Hamann makes no important distinction between the Berlin rationalism and Kantianism, and that therefore his "herculean task" includes the refutation of the latter as well as of the former. The call to experience is the call to verbal experience, not to the verbal experience of man in isolation, but of man in relation to the scripturally mediated divine Logos. Further, "nominalism" or the capacity of the mind of invent names for relations is seen as the freedom which language grants to man, a freedom which may be abused by application of the dissolving acids of reason. It is apparent that he looked to natural language for a demonstration of the structure of reality. Here we find the most likely source of his peculiar unconcern for system[56] precisely in what he aptly termed the "philosophical century." (II,179).

The struggle of the rationalist to free himself from experience—a struggle which Hamann saw epitomized in Lessing and Kant—consists in the effort to free himself from the conditions which are binding upon reason. These conditions are best demonstrated by an appeal to natural language, for a single sentence of natural language[57] is a demonstration of the "transfer and *communicatio idiomatum* of the mental and material, of extension and mind, of body and thought." Nature, "whose Lord and Founder is a Spirit" (G,V,495) is faithfully reflected in language, and it is the natural conditions of knowledge, symbolically revealed in language, which the rationalist seeks to circumvent. As the result of our investigation, the relation of the "empty" words of natural language to the words referring to objects may serve as the clue to a better understanding of Hamann's conception of the relation of reason to experience. What need for an artificially constructed organon or criterion of the relation of reason to experience, Hamann asked in effect, when the organon or criterion is present before our very eyes? The subordination of syntactical or relational symbolism to objective symbolism in natural language renders manifest why reason should be "the servant, and not the law-giver of nature." (G,V,16).

From the theological standpoint, the most important implication of our findings—and one which suggests a fruitful area of research beyond the scope of this study—is the opportunity it affords for a better understanding of Hamann's conception of the relation of faith and reason.[58] For, if our interpretation be correct, it should be possible to point to natural language as a "parable" of this relation. On this interpretation, Hamann would seem to say that since there can be no meaningful utterances in natural language without the presence of the discrete symbols we have been discussing, either explicitly or implicitly, likewise there can be no religious knowledge without both faith and reason. Reason held to its proper domain can no more conflict with faith than, for instance, a preposition or an adverb can conflict with a substantive in ordinary language. If a conflict takes place between them, it can only mean that one type of symbol is encroaching upon the domain of the other. This is what Hamann seems to imply, when he describes abstractions as relations.

To proceed on the basis of faith alone as in the case of Tertullianism,[59] or virtually on the basis of reason alone, as in the case of Averroism,[60] is comparable to speaking in unipolar rather than in the bipolar symbolism of natural language. Tertullianism would be comparable to a discourse entirely in the symbolism of objects, and Averroism to a discourse entirely in the symbolism of relations. The manner in which such a procedure can be rendered graphic we have previously discussed.

In spite of his antirationalism, Hamann recognizes the necessity for the cooperation of faith and reason in all knowledge, but especially in religious knowledge. Neither is, in isolation, an absolute good.[61]

> Reason is the source of all truth and of all errors. It is the tree of the knowledge of good and evil. Therefore, both parties are right and both are wrong which deify it and blaspheme it. Faith likewise is the source of unfaith and of superstition. 'Out of the same mouth proceedeth blessing and cursing.' (G, V, 513).

Statements to the effect that "faith needs reason just as much as the latter needs the former" (G,V,504), may be predicated of language as well as of the specific problem of the relation of faith and reason, for, as we have noted, both faith and reason are essential elements of cognition symbolically present in language before the excessive intervention of reason eliminates faith and its peculiar symbolism.

Our investigation in this chapter has shown that Hamann held excessive ratiocination to issue in a "reworking" of natural language into abstract form, and that this process, inaugurated by the desire of the abstract thinker to attain complete autonomy, issues in a destruction of the functional duality in unity of language. The philosophies of Lessing and Kant were seen as classic expressions of this tendency, even though the rationalism of each was ostensibly more cautious than that of their predecessors in the German Enlightenment. The opportunity which natural language affords of studying in concrete form the proper relation of reason and experience or of reason and faith is neglected by the abstract thinker. He thus has no adequate criterion by which to judge the proper union of these disparate elements of cognition.

Russell has said of Leibniz that he "drew inferences from syntax to the real world."[62] Hamann, we may be sure, would agree but would retort that this is precisely the difficulty, for the abstract thinker deals in "mere relations" or in "relations without things," and, from the linguistic standpoint, these are to be equated with the syntactical symbols of ordinary language in isolation from symbols referring to objects. But this, according to Hamann, is understood only on the basis of an appeal to natural language. "He who does not enter into the womb of *language*," he wrote, "which is the *Deipara of our reason, is not adept for the baptism* of a church and state reformation." (H.'s italics. VI,39). For only thereby can he understand the final results of the abstract transformation of language. Hamann's unwaveringly hostile attitude toward the abstracting process is nowhere better expressed than in *Aesthetics in a Nutshell*:

> O for a muse like the fire of a goldsmith and like the soap of the fullers!—She will dare to cleanse the *natural use of the senses* from the *unnatural use of abstractions*, by which our *concepts* of things are just as mutilated as the name of the Creator is *suppressed* and blasphemed. (H.'s italics. II, 283-284).

## CHAPTER V

## SUMMARY AND CONCLUSION

Our investigation in this study has established that language and thought are inextricably intertwined for Hamann, and that he conceived the abstracting processes of reason to consist essentially in an excessive functioning of the purely reflective capacities of the mind with the resultant expansion of the purely relational symbolism of ordinary language. According to Hamann, the aim of the rationalist is to render reason autonomous or independent of experience. Although this goal is impossible of attainment, it is possible for reason to achieve a partial divorce from experience by transforming natural language into abstract language. But the consequence of the reworking of natural language into the abstract form is twofold. Substantives and adjectives no longer refer to real objects and real qualities, but to "fancies," and, further, language has been divested of its ability to appeal to the imaginative and emotional life of man. This latter consequence is spiritually quite deleterious, since man is conceived as a primarily emotional being. Thus, language which is, properly speaking, the "mother of reason and revelation," may become, by virtue of its ability to multiply abstractions inordinately, "the center of the misunderstanding of reason with itself."

It was further found that the concept of the sense-unit as the indivisible category of language is everywhere implied in Hamann's verbalistic philosophy, and that the sense-unit, when considered objectively, always involves the peculiar symbolism of relations and objects, and, when considered subjectively, involves the reflective and perceptive processes of the mind in a functional union, which Hamann terms "the finest parable of the hypostatic union of the sensory and rational natures, of the mutual idiom-exchange of their powers." Our findings with regard to the reality of relations in Hamann's thought add weight to his own description of his philosophy as "historical and physical realism," if the term "physical" is understood in the Hamannian sense. For his assertion of the dependence of the mind upon experience for the initial knowledge of the fundamental relations of space and time suggests a thoroughgoing and radical empiricism, and also suggests important differences between the Magus and Kant. Although the former's assumption of the reality of objects and the reality of relations places him in a philosophically difficult position, he does not feel the full force of the dilemma because of the unsystematic nature of his thought. Whatever the ontological status of relations may be, the all-important fact for Hamann is that language is the bearer of discrete types of symbols which can best be differentiated on the basis of the perceptive and reflective processes of the mind or on the basis of objects and relations. Since his thought tends to press all reality into the mold of immediately intuited objects and relations, the subject of the actual status of properties or qualities is ignored.

From the purely metaphysical standpoint, Hamann's language theory cannot logically provide the basis for a monistic view of the universe. Indeed, it would suggest rather a pluralistic view. For the only rational clue to the nature of reality is furnished by the bipolar categories of language, and if the analogy of language is followed, every larger real entity would be capable of dissolution into smaller and smaller entities until indivisible ones were reached. This must be so, because every larger unit of language is susceptible of dissolution into smaller and smaller units, and this process may continue until the categories or elementary sense-units of language have been reached. It is true that this unit is characterized by an indestructible duality in unity, and, in so far as this is true, Hamann's language philosophy provides some rational basis for a monistic system. But even with the assumption of the absolutely bipolar nature of the linguistic categories and their correspondents in reality, one would still have to embark upon something like the Hegelian dialectic to arrive at a metaphysical monism. Again an appeal to the nature of language makes this plain. Unlike the Kantian categories, the number of the categories or sense-units of language, hence of reality, is infinite, and the unity of larger, metaphysical wholes cannot be predicated on the basis of their unity alone. To construct a genuinely monistic system on such a basis would involve a procedure quite alien to Hamann's basic principles.

That the categories of language did, however, provide Hamann with a basis for a philosophy of unity was the result of his religious faith. On the basis of faith, the togetherness of the discrete components of cognition and of the discrete components of reality, symbolized in language, became for him a "parable" of the ultimate unity of all reality. Therefore, the togetherness of these discrete elements in all meaningful statements is, from the metaphysical and theological standpoints, the most important unity in experience, and is imparted by the creative act of God, not by any human powers. On this subject Hamann could say, "To dissect a body and an event into its first elements means to desire to detect God's invisible being, his eternal power and Godhead." For Hamann the unity of the world is ultimately a creational unity.

It should be recalled that even the linguistic category demands faith for its acceptance. For such a unit must always contain reference to real objects of immediate experience, and the perception of objects requires, according to Hamann, faith. Moreover, the functional synthesis of the discrete types of symbols in language is a fact of experience also, and as such must likewise be accepted on the basis of faith. Kant could ignore faith in his theory of pure reason only because his transcendentalism seeks to transcend or to go beyond experience. But the importance of faith in all cognition—which Hamann might establish partly with the aid of Hume—still does not lead him beyond the pluralism which we have mentioned. For even the successful establishment of the categories of language as the categories of thought would leave him with the implication of an infinite number of indestructible unities and not with one all-embracing unity. Something more than the faith which supports the categories of language is necessary for the acceptance of the unity of all reality. Again it is the transcendent unity of God which provides the basis for the belief in the unity of all reality.[1]

Further, Hamann's linguistic philosophy does not escape the epistemological dualism which is characteristic of much of Western philosophy. Although his thought, as I have understood it, requires a reconceiving of both elements in the dualism of mind and experience so that the former is characterized by the ability to reflect and to perceive and the latter by a dichotomy into relations and objects, they are in the last analysis to be regarded as distinct from, and parallel to one another. This makes it difficult, but not impossible to deal with his thought in terms of the subject-object dualism. The broad distinction between mind and experience—whose interrelations are ambiguous— reveals that, at least on this score, there is no fundamental difference between his epistemology and that of the Cartesians, despite his vigorous demurrer.

Likewise, the synthesis of the discrete functions of the mind and the synthesis of objects and relations would appear logically to demand an epistemological dualism. For obviously the synthesis of the discrete symbols of language is accomplished by the mind, and Hamann recognizes this frequently enough to justify Unger's speaking of the "inner nature of the speaker" as descriptive of this power. Although some of Hamann's terms for this capacity such as the "transcendental root" of reflection and perception are non-committal, many expressions like "hypostatic union" and *shekinah* attest the religious attitude he adopted toward it and his unwillingness to regard it as interior to the mind. Strictly speaking, however, one must consider it as the mental counterpart of the togetherness of relations and objects in experience. In such a case, it would be the equivalent of the "productive imagination" of the German idealists. But we may be sure that Hamann would not admit this possibility, for his tendency was to escape the dualism implied in his thought by assimilating mind to experience, a tendency in which he was strengthened by his theocentric religious philosophy and by the empiricism of certain British thinkers. However, there is reason to believe that Hamann's reconceiving of the nature of mind and of experience has certain virtues, especially from the standpoint of linguistic philosophy. Hence, the theoretical dualism ultimately implied in his epistemology does not argue that he has nothing to say in this connection.

Hamann's extreme aversion to abstraction made him the unwavering leader of the anti-rationalistic foes of the German Enlightenment in the third quarter of the eighteenth century. This hostility became a source of strength not only for him, but also for his followers. On the other hand, it caused him to be singularly unappreciative of the virtues of more abstract thinkers. Although it is always clear that his strictures were directed against scientific philosophy and not against science itself, the actual status of science in his thought is thoroughly ambiguous.

## SUMMARY AND CONCLUSION 99

With the one exception of linguistic science, it must be conceded that his attitude toward the scientific spirit in general is hostile. The ambitious claims of the pre-Kantian Enlighteners, however, render his attitude somewhat more understandable, if not defensible. Finally, it should be recognized that he was inconsistent in decrying abstraction, while proceeding to construct a theory of language which, however it be understood, is essentially abstract.

Hamann failed to take the step which we have found to be implied in his verbalistic philosophy, namely, the identification of the relational symbols of ordinary language as the archetypes of abstractions. But, as I believe to have demonstrated, this identification is a justifiable deduction from his general principles, and it illuminates his specific utterances on the nature of language. Such an interpretation reveals in his linguistic philosophy a structural coherence which is otherwise hidden. Since it requires an appeal to linguistic facts as normative, it does not set up an abstract principle as explanatory of his thought—a procedure which would be in manifest opposition to his spirit.

Hamann's recurrent feeling of optimism about the language theory is evidence, in my opinion, of his vague awareness of a possibility at this point. This optimistic feeling, however, alternated with profound pessimism about the same subject. "If I were as eloquent as Demosthenes," he wrote to Herder in 1784, "I would do no more than repeat one sentence three times: Reason is language, Logos. On this marrow-bone I gnaw, and I shall gnaw myself to death on it. There still remains darkness upon the face of this deep for me; I still wait for an apocalyptic angel with a key to this abyss."[2] The apocalyptic angel with a key to the abyss has not yet appeared, but I believe that it is possible, strictly on the basis of Hamann's own general principles and in conformity with his spirit, to attain to a better understanding of his thought on this important subject.

Whether or not the outline of Hamann's verbalistic philosophy presented in this study may finally prove justified, one thing at least appears certain: No account of his philosophy which ignores the linking of abstractions with relations and which fails to investigate his covert doctrine of relations will be able to do full justice to his thought. If in the light of its testing in various areas of Hamann's thought and in the light of a thorough examination of the published material which will become available in the next few years, the present interpretation of Hamann's concept of linguistic unity be finally called in question, attention has at least been called to the need for a serious consideration of the doctrines examined.

## NOTES TO INTRODUCTION

1. Johann Wolfgang von Goethe, *The Autobiography of Goethe*, trans. John Oxenford (London, 1848), I, 446-447.
2. Johann Georg Hamann, *Schriften*, eds. Friedrich Roth and Gustaf A. Wiener (Berlin, 1824), V, 171. Since the edition of Roth and Wiener is the principal source cited in this study, brief references to it shall hereinafter be inserted parenthetically in the text. A Roman numeral is used to designate the volume number, an Arabic numeral to designate the page number.
3. Hamann, IV, 45; cf. I, 52; IV, 439; VI, 49-50; VII, 10-11, 34-35. Cf. also Johann Georg Hamann, *J. G. Hamanns, des Magus im Norden, Leben und Schriften*, ed. C. H. Gildemeister (Gotha, 1868), V. 385, 496. The last cited work also affords source material, and references to it shall be treated like references to the Roth-Wiener edition with the letter "G" designating Gildemeister's work. The fifth volume of this work is particularly important, since it is the only currently available source of Hamann's correspondence with Friedrich Heinrich Jacobi (1743-1819).
4. See Arnold Kowalewski, "Hamann als religiöser Lebensphilosoph," *Bilder aus dem religiösen und kirchlichen Leben Ostpreussens* (Königsberg, 1927), pp. 55-78.
5. See Erwin Metzke, *J. G. Hamanns Stellung in der Philosophie des 18. Jahrhunderts* (Halle/Saale, 1934), pp. 87 ff., 121 ff.; Tage Schack, *Johann Georg Hamann* (Copenhagen, 1948), *passim*; Walter Lowrie, *Johann Georg Hamann: An Existentialist* (Princeton, 1950), p. 9. This noteworthy and readable introduction to Hamann's life and work came to my attention after the present study was substantially completed. I shall have occasion, however, to comment briefly on Lowrie's general characterization of Hamann's philosophy, *infra*, p. 105; Philip Merlan, "From Hume to Hamann," *The Personalist*, XXXII, No. 1 (Winter, January, 1951), 16. This writer sees in Goethe's characterization of Hamann "the seeds of some of the most interesting doctrines of existentialism."
6. Rudolf Unger, *Hamann und die Aufklärung* (Jena, 1911), I, 240 ff.
7. Metzke, *op. cit.*, p. 88.
8. See Rudolf Unger, *Hamanns Sprachtheorie im Zusammenhang seines Denkens* (Munich, 1905). This work shall hereinafter be cited by the short title, *Sprachtheorie*. Discussions of Hamann's language theory may also be found in: Erik Peterson, "Das Problem der Bibelauslegung im Pietismus des 18. Jahrhunderts," *Zeitschrift für systematische Theologie*, I (1923), 486-481; Carl Dyrssen, "Hamann und Oetinger," *Zeitwende*, I (1925), 376-396; Fritz Blanke, "Gottessprache und Menschensprache bei J. G. Hamann," *Theologische Blätter*, IX, No. 8 (August, 1930), cols. 201-210; Metzke, *op. cit.*, pp. 123-132. The following writers have dealt with Hamann's language theory within the framework of larger historical studies: H. Steinthal, *Der Ursprung der Sprache* (Berlin, 1851), pp. 42-59; Fritz Mauthner, *Beiträge zu einer Kritik der Sprache* (3d. ed.; Stuttgart, 1912), Vol. I, *passim*. Ernst Cassirer, *Die Philosophie der symbolischen Formen* (Berlin, 1923), I, 158 ff. Many philologists and linguistic philosophers fail to mention Hamann at all, despite the fact that they assign an important place to the linguistic philosophy of Hamann's disciple, Herder. Typical illustrations of this may be found in: Otto Jespersen, *Language: Its Nature, Development, and Origin* (New York, 1925), pp. 27 ff; Karl Vossler, *The Spirit of Language in Civilization*, trans. Oscar Oeser (New York, 1932), p. 30; Richard Albert Wilson, *The Miraculous Birth of Language* (New York, 1948), *passim*.

9. Cf. Hamann, I, 413, 481; II, 12; VI, 64.
10. Johann Georg Hamann, *Neue Hamanniana*, ed. Heinrich Weber (Munich, 1905), p. 105.
11. Cassirer, *Die Philosophie der symbolischen Formen*, p. 92.
12. Unger, *Hamann und die Aufklärung*, I, 14. 152.
13. Hermann Hettner, *Geschichte der deutschen Literatur im achtzehnten Jahrhundert*, ed. Georg Witkowski (Leipzig, 1928), Part III, p. 181. Cf. also the adverse criticism of the Magus in G. G. Gervinus, *Geschichte der deutschen Dichtung*, ed. Karl Bartsch (5th ed.; Leipzig, 1873), IV, 487-504.
14. Jakob Minor, *Johann Georg Hamann in seiner Bedeutung für die Sturm- und Drangperiode* (Frankfurt am Main, 1881), p. 2.
15. For an excellent summary of the relations of Goethe and Hamann, see Josef Nadler, *Die Hamannausgabe* (Halle/Saale, 1930), pp. 91 ff.
16. See Minor, *op. cit., passim*.
17. See Hans Emil Weber, "Zwei Propheten des Irrationalismus," *Neue kirchliche Zeitschrift*, XXVIII (1917), 23-58, 77-125; Wilhelm Rodemann, *Hamann und Kierkegaard* (Gütersloh, 1922); Rudolf Unger, "Hamann und die Empfindsamkeit," *Euphorion*, XXX (1929), 169-170; Walter Lowrie, *Kierkegaard* (London, 1938), pp. 164-166, and *Johann Georg Hamann: An Existentialist, passim*; Pierre Klossowski, *Les Méditations Bibliques de Hamann* (Paris: 1948), pp. 9-117; Jean Wahl, *Études Kierkegaardiennes* (2d ed.; Paris, 1949), pp. 418ff. Some writers warn against the interpretation of Hamann in terms of his influence on Kierkegaard and the existentialists. See Käte Nadler, "Hamann und Hegel: Zum Verhältnis von Dialektik und Existentialität," *Logos*, XX (1931), 275, Kurt Leese, *Krisis und Wende des christlichen Geistes* (2d. rev. ed.; Berlin, 1941) and Marie Theres Küsters, *Inhaltsanalyse von J. Georg Hamanns Aesthetica in Nuce* (Bottrop, Westphalia, 1936), p. 74. Students of the Hamann-Kierkegaard relationship will be grateful for Lowrie's listing of all Kierkegaard's references to Hamann in *Johann Georg Hamann: An Existentialist*, p. 4.
18. See Rudolf Unger, "Johann Georg Hamann," *Die Grossen Deutschen: neue Deutsche Biographie*, eds. Willy Andreas and Wilhelm von Scholz (Berlin, 1935), II, 277-289.
19. Johann Georg Hamann, *Sämtliche Werke*, ed. Josef Nadler (Vienna, 1949-1950), Vols. I, II.
20. At present the source material available to students of Hamann is limited chiefly to those of his writings contained in the cited edition of Roth and Wiener, the fifth volume of Gildemeister's work, already cited, various items of Hamanniana published by Kleuker (1837), Funck (1894), Konschel (1905), Weber (1905), already cited, Schmitz-Kallenberg (1917), and the first two volumes of Nadler's recent edition mentioned above.
21. Johann Wolfgang von Goethe, *Sämtliche Werke* (Jubiläumsausgabe; Stuttgart, [n.d.], XXIV, 81.
22. Even the monumental work by Unger, *Hamann und die Aufklärung*, is based almost exclusively on material published at the time of its writing. See *ibid.*, I, 17.
23. Josef Nadler, *Johann Georg Hamann: der Zeuge des Corpus Mysticum* (Salzburg, 1949).
24. See Hamann, I, 442; VI, 151-152.
25. G. W. F. Hegel, *Werke* (Complete ed.; Berlin, 1835) XVII, 74.
26. Søren Kierkegaard, *Concluding Unscientific Postscript*, trans. David F. Swenson (Princeton, 1944), p. 224. Cf. Hamann's remark to Jacobi, G, V, 495.
27. See Gunther Ipsen, *Sprachphilosophie der Gegenwart* (Berlin, 1930),

especially pp. 21 ff. Cf. further Wilbur Marshall Urban, *Language and Reality* (London, 1939), *passim.*
28. Hamann, G, IV, 7. Cf. also Johann Georg Hamann, *Schriften J. G. Hamanns*, ed. Karl Widmaier (Leipzig, 1921), pp. 323-324; Hamann, V, 257. Apparently the only extensive research on Hamann now in progress in the United States is a study of the Magus' style. T. C. Tatman is preparing a dissertation at the University of Pennsylvania entitled, "Study of the Language of Hamann before and after 1758." See *Publications of the Modern Language Association*, LXVI, No. 3 (April, 1951), 250.
29. Hegel, *op. cit.*, p. 44.
30. The only work by Hamann available in English at the present time is a translation of the *Beilage zu Dangeuils Anmerkungen über die Vorteile und Nachteile von Frankreich und Grossbrittanien in Ansehung des Handels und der übrigen Quellen von der Macht der Staaten* (1756) entitled "The Merchant." See *Prose Writers of Germany*, ed. Frederic Hedge (4th ed.; New York, 1856), pp. 121-127. A series of quotations from Hamann pertaining to pedagogical theory appear in Karl von Raumer, "Johann Georg Hamann," *American Journal of Education*, XI (1859), 247-259.

## NOTES TO CHAPTER I

1. Unger, *Sprachtheorie*, p. 255. Cf. Unger, "Einführung," *Johann Georg Hamann: Sibyllinische Blätter des Magus* (Jena and Leipzig, 1905), p. xvi.
2. Unger, *Sprachtheorie*, p. 255.
3. For example, Josef Nadler terms the language theory the "root" of the Hamann problem. *Die Hamannausgabe*, p. 158.
4. Hegel, *op. cit.*, p. 44.
5. See Unger, *Sprachtheorie*, pp. 7, 8 ,9, 20, 255; *Hamann und die Aufklärung*, I, 205, 317, 574, 575. Friedrich Burschell flatly states that Hegel's principles for the interpretation of Hamann are the correct ones. See "Ueber Johann Georg Hamann," *Logos*, IV (1913), 103.
6. Metzke, *op. cit.*, p. 1.
7. See Theodor Heckel, *Johann Georg Hamann: Briefe zur Einführung in Leben und Theologie* (Göttingen, 1947), p. 1.
8. Goethe, *Sämtliche Werke*, XXVI, 224.
9. Hamann would doubtless feel that there is an element of ironic justice in the conclusion of contemporary form-critics that "the recognition of the poetic structure in practically all Jesus' sayings" is imperative in the criticism of the Gospels. For the form-critics are the direct heirs of the mantle of men like Michaelis and Reimarus. See Frederick C. Grant, "Form Criticism," *An Encyclopedia of Religion*, ed. V. Ferm (New York, 1945), p. 285.
10. See Blanke, "Gottessprache und Menschensprache bei Johann Georg Hamann," col. 202.
11. For a study of Michaelis as a Biblical scholar, see my article, "J. D. Michaelis: Rational Biblicist," *Journal of English and Germanic Philology*, XLIX, No. 2 (April, 1950), 172-181.
12. Ernst Cassirer, *Idee und Gestalt* (Berlin, 1921), p. 74.
13. Hamann, G, V, 51; cf. 16; II, 271-272, 421, 432, 437, 443 ff; VII, 404.
14. I employ the term "natural language" as opposed to "abstract language" despite the fact that Hamann sometimes applied the term "natural language" to abstract language, especially when he had in mind the analogy between natural religion as the invention of human reason and purely rational language as the same. See Hamann, VI, 143. In spite

of the ambiguity of the term "natural," it appears to be the best available for our purposes, and it is always used in this study in the Hamannian sense of nature conceived as unspoiled by the excessive intervention of reason, as the "language of nature" about which he speaks in the *Aesthetica in nuce.* See II, 293.
15. Hamann, IV, 262. For the idea of nature as a "text" or "book" the meaning of which is ultimately divine, see: I, 86, 88, 131, 148, 499, 508, 509; II, 19, 236, 274, 276, 285, 293, 300; IV, 33; VI, 113.
16. Goethe, *Maximen und Reflexionen.* Quoted by Cassirer, *Idee und Gestalt,* p. 30.
17. W. Windelband, *A History of Philosophy,* trans. James H. Tufts (2d. ed., New York, 1923), p. 510.
18. Hermann Bauke, *Die Probleme der Theologie Calvins* (Leipzig, 1922), pp. 13 ff.
19. H. Kraemer, *The Christian Message in a Non-Christian World* (London, 1937), p. 117.
20. Blanke, "Gottessprache und Menschensprache bei J. G. Hamann," col. 202.
21. See Agathe H. F. Thornton, "The Hebrew Conception of Speech as Creative Energy," *Hibbert Journal,* XLIV, No. 2 (January, 1946), 133.
22. In the *Beilage zu Dangeuils Anmerkungen* (1756) Hamann espouses ideas typical of the Enlightenment. For a treatment of the place of this essay in intellectual history, see Philip Merlan, "Parva Hamanniana: Hamann as Spokesman of the Middle Class," *Journal of the History of Ideas,* IX, No. 3 (June, 1948), 380-384.
23. Burschell well expresses this idea, *op. cit.,* p. 101.
24. Although these words were directed not against the French Academy but against the rationalistic Biblical interpreters, they may apply here, for Hamann makes no distinction between the language reformers' attempted control of language and the rationalistic reworking of language in the interest of philosophy.
25. See Unger, *Sprachtheorie,* p. 247.
26. Otto Jespersen says of the dictionaries of the French and Italian Academies that they were "less descriptions of actual usage than prescriptions for the best usage of words." *Language: Its Nature, Development, and Origin,* p. 25.
27. From a remark made to Hippel. See Theodor Gottlieb Hippel, *Biographie des königlichen preussischen Geheimenkriegsrats zu Königsberg Theodor Gottlieb von Hippel,* ed. Schlichtegroll (Gotha, 1801), pp. 285-286.
28. Hamann, VI, 34-35. Hamann was well aware of the comprehensiveness of his idea of language. See II, 128.
29. The large number of works on linguistics in Hamann's private library yields some insight into the importance of the subject for him. See Nora Imendörffer, *Johann Georg Hamann und seine Bücherei* (Königsberg, 1938), pp. 132 ff.
30. For a review of Hamann's achievements in foreign language study, see Josef Nadler, *Die Hamannausgabe,* pp. 8-11, 176-177.
31. It is erroneous to say of Hamann, as one writer does, that "it is with words *as words* (S.'s italics) that his chief concern lies." Nor is this statement atoned for by the fact that its author recognizes elsewhere the profound philosophical and religious implications of Hamann's striving with the *word.* See Ronald Gregor Smith, "The Living and Speaking God: A Study of Hamann's Doctrine of 'the Word,'" *The Hibbert Journal,* XLII, No. 3 (April, 1944), 198.
32. Josef Nadler, *Die Hamannausgabe,* p. 9.

33. Hamann, II, 62; III, 333; VII, 238.
34. Hamann ascribes this principle to Luther in a letter to his brother in 1760 in which he relies upon J. A. Bengel for its authenticity. For a discussion of Luther as the source of the expression, see Paul Ernst, *Hamann und Bengel* (Königsberg, 1935), pp. 74-76.
35. Hamann, G, V, 509; Cf. 22; II, 135; III, 15-16.
36. Hettner, op. cit., Part III, pp. 182-183.
37. Unger, *Sprachtheorie*, p. 153.
38. The term "sense-unit" is borrowed from Jespersen, though he does not especially recommend it. As used in this study, however, it is always understood as defined in the text. For a discussion of the "sense-unit" as a problem for the grammarian, see Otto Jespersen, *The Philosophy of Grammar* (London, 1925), pp. 92-95.
39. See Hamann II, 135; IV, 193; VI, 25, 365; VII, 6, 9, 216; G, V, 7, 422. Hamann acknowledged his debt to Edward Young for these terms, II, 135; VII, 216. See also line 469 of Young's *Night Thoughts*.
40. Unger, *Sprachtheorie*, p. 151.
41. Walter Lowrie sees in this aspect of Hamann's thought a "Christian existentialism." "As an existentialist Hamann laid emphasis upon the bodily man, the man of flesh and blood . . . . therefore man's response to God must be a response of the whole man, of his passions as well as his intellect—faith is love and practical obedience." Lowrie, *Johann Georg Hamann: An Existentialist*, p. 9. If no more is meant by ascribing existentialism to Hamann than this, one may concur in the ascription. But one may not therefore conclude that Hamann always made a cult of the paradox. Hamann believed that a clear understanding of the structure of language would reveal to what extent the human mind is capable of developing a rationale of faith. It would also reveal the reason why intellection and emotion may not be separated in the process of cognition.
42. Urban, op. cit., p. 21.

## NOTES TO CHAPTER II

1. Alfred North Whitehead, *Symbolism* (New York, 1927), p. 16.
2. See Hamann, IV, 146; VI, 183, 301; VII, 414; G, V, 49.
3. See Metzke, op. cit., p. 53.
4. There is a discrepancy between the positions of Plato as stated in the *Cratylus* and in the *Seventh Epistle*. The statement from the latter that "no intelligent man will ever be so bold as to put in language those things which his reason has contemplated," is taken here as generally definitive of his real position. See Urban, op. cit., p. 53.
5. See especially secs. 21, 22 of George Berkeley's *A Treatise Concerning the Principles of Human Knowledge*.
6. See especially Joseph Stalin, "On Several Problems of Linguistics," *The Soviet Linguistic Controversy*, trans. John V. Murra et al. (New York, 1951), pp. 86-87.
7. Although Descartes did not address himself extensively to this problem, his thought on the subject is clear from the letter to Mersenne of November 20, 1629.
8. See especially Bertrand Russell, *The Scientific Outlook* (New York, 1931), p. 82.
9. See especially Alfred North Whitehead, *Process and Reality* (New York, 1930), p. 16.
10. That Kant did not deal consciously with the problem of language is conceded by A. C. Ewing, who writes that "linguistics play no conscious

part in Kant's philosophy." "Kantianism," *Twentieth Century Philosophy* (New York, 1943), p. 259. Cf. further the statement that Kant's *Critique of Pure Reason* "in general suffers throughout from a lack of a critical study of language." Urban, *op. cit.*, p. 158.
11. John B. Watson, *Behaviorism* (New York, 1925), p. 191.
12. Perhaps the source of this tendency is also to be sought in pragmatism. See, for example, C. S. Peirce, *The Philosophy of Peirce*, ed. Justus Buchler (New York, 1940), p. 258.
13. Ewing, *op. cit.*, p. 259.
14. E.g., Hamann, II, 316.
15. See Cassirer, *Die Philosophie der symbolischen Formen*, I, 73-89.
16. E.g., Hamann, II, 262; IV, 193; VII, 6, 9, 216; G, V, 422.
17. The transition from the creative divine speech to the speech of human beings is a crucial point in Hamann's theory of language. Hugo Delff has suggested that the link between the divine and human speech is to be found in the idea of *imago dei*. "Johann Georg Hamann," *Allgemeine Deutsche Biographie*, Vol. X (1879), 463.
18. E.g., Hamann, IV, 23; VI, 34, 170; VII, 12.
19. Hamann, (unpublished item from Roth's *Nachlass*). Quoted by Metzke, *op. cit.*, p. 42.
20. Hamann, VII, 59. The gulf between God and man can be bridged only by drastic action on the part of God. See VII, 41; G, V, 51.
21. H. A. Korff, *Geist der Goethezeit* (Leipzig, 1923), I, 108. Cf. Unger, *Hamann und die Aufklärung* I, 108.
22. Josef Nadler, *Hamann, Kant, Goethe* (Halle/Saale, 1931), p. 6. When one is inclined to find mysticism, he finds it in strange places. Thus F. J. Schmitz finds common elements of mysticism in Lessing and Hamann. The mysticism which these two men have in common requires a definition. See F. J. Schmitz, *The Problem of Individualism and the Crises in the Lives of Lessing and Hamann* (Los Angeles, 1944), p. 144.
23. Hamann, I, 99. Cf. Metzke, *op. cit.*, pp. 133 ff.
24. See John Wright Buckham, "Mysticism," An *Encyclopedia of Religion*, p. 513. Richard E. Benz's likening of Hamann's mysticism to that of Johann Sebastian Bach appears to me to be justified. See *Sprach- und Volkserlebnis bei Hamann und Herder*. Sonderdruck aus der wissenschaftlichen Festschrift zur 700 Jahr-Feier der Kreuzschule zu Dresden, 1926, p. 131. For a discussion of the parallel between Blake and Hamann, see Helene Richter, "Blake und Hamann," *Archiv für das Studium der neueren Sprachen und Literaturen*, CLVIII (1930), 213-221, CLIX (1931), 36-45, 195-210. Miss Richter comes to the following suggestive conclusion: "Zieht man nun das Fazit aus beider Leben, so mutet Blake beinahe wie die Erfüllung von Hamanns Daseinstraum an." *Ibid.*, p. 210.
25. Hamann never utilized the speculative mystics as sources for his thought. For his opinion of Böhme see I, 539; II, 77; III, 199-200; V. 179. Kurt Leese is doubtless correct when he asserts that Hamann was essentially independent of Böhme *op. cit.*, p. 181. Hamann was even less sympathetic to Swedenborg. See VII, 179, 348. For representative discussions of Hamann's mysticism, see, in addition to work cited, Heinrich Weber, *Hamann und Kant* (Munich, 1904), pp. 169 ff.; Unger, *Sprachtheorie*, pp. 76 ff., 99 ff., also *Hamann und die Aufklärung*, I, 160 ff.; Wilhelm Lütgert, *Die Religion des deutschen Idealismus und ihr Ende* Gütersloh, 1923), II, 3-4; Dyrssen, *op. cit.*; Helmuth Schreiner, *Die Menschwerdung Gottes in der Theologie Johann Georg Hamanns* (Stuttgart, 1946), pp. 26 ff.; Josef Nadler, *Johann Georg Hamann: der Zeuge des Corpus Mysticum*, passim.
26. G. W. Leibniz, *The Monadology*, trans. Robert Latta (London, 1948), p. 29.

27. G. W. Leibniz, *Principles of Nature and of Grace*, par. 5. Quoted by Latta, Leibniz, *The Monadology*, p. 234.
28. See Latta's summary of Leibniz's doctrine of innate principles, *ibid.*, pp. 233-234.
29. Unger, *Hamann und die Aufklärung*, I, 10.
30. Latta, in Leibniz, *The Monadology*, p. 234.
31. See Unger, *Hamann und die Aufklärung*, I, 288 ff. Although acquainted with Shaftesbury and Hutcheson before writing the *Sokratische Denkwürdigkeiten*, Hamann cannot be shown to have been influenced by them as by Young, who, however, is not definitive for the genius-concept. It is true that Young's *Conjectures on Original Composition* appeared in the spring of 1759 and that the *Denkwürdigkeiten* was not begun until August of that year, but according to Unger there is no reason to assume that Hamann had read Young's work before writing the essay in question. *Ibid.* Kind, in spite of his demonstration of the considerable parallelism between Young's thoughts on genius and orginality and Hamann's thoughts on the same, does not prove Hamann's dependence upon Young in this matter. He furnishes no evidence that Hamann actually read the *Conjectures* before August, 1759. Therefore, his statement that Hamann "in his views on originality and individualism, owes the greater part of his material to Young" must be questioned. See John L. Kind, *Edward Young in Germany* (New York, 1906), pp. 33-40.
32. It is this unusual synthesis of religio-cultural interests that caused Hamann to be "wie Shakespeares so auch Luthers erster Prophet im modernen Geistesleben." Horst Stephan, "Ein Ahnherr des modernen Christentums," *Die Christliche Welt*, XVI, No. 36 (September 4, 1902), col. 854.
33. Hamann's fame as a literary critic is securely established. For specialized studies of his critical activity, see: Edith Säemann, *J. G. Hamann und die französische Literatur* (Königsberg, 1931); Walter Hilpert, *Johann Georg Hamann als Kritiker der deutschen Literatur* (Königsberg, 1933). American scholarship has stressed this side of Hamann. See Robert T. Clark, "Hamann's Opinion of Herder's *Ursachen des gesunkenen Geschmacks*," *Modern Language Notes*, LXI, No. 2 (February, 1946), 94-99; Francis Andrew Brown, "Hamann's Opinion of Muralt," *Journal of English and Germanic Philology*, XLVII, No. 1 (January, 1948), 53-58.
34. Minor, *op. cit.*, p. 3.
35. Hamann's own procedure exemplifies this principle. Unger gives a list of some of the obsolete and obsolescent words which Hamann revived. *Sprachtheorie*, pp. 247-248.
36. Occasionally Hamann lapses from this position with reference to the adequacy of language to express the feelings. See Hamann, V, 258.
37. Delff stresses this aspect of Hamann's thought, *op. cit.*, p. 463.

## NOTES TO CHAPTER III

1. Metzke, *op. cit.* p. 126.
2. A recent investigator of Hamann's theology devotes only five pages out of 334 to the problem of reason and language. See E. Jansen Schoonhoven, *Natur en Genade bij J. G. Hamann* (Nijkerk, 1945), pp. 262-266. In a review of Lowrie's *Johann Georg Hamann: An Existentialist*, Montgomery Belgion censures the author for his neglect of the language problem in the study. See *Theology*, LIV, No. 376 (October, 1951), 390. The Danish writer, Tage Schack, martyred by the Germans in 1945 during their occupation of Denmark, had, however, planned a chapter on reason and language in the projected second volume of his Hamann-work. See Schack, *op. cit.*, p. 337.

3. Metzke, *op. cit.*, pp. 38 ff., 126 ff.
4. From *Three Philosophical Poets*. Quoted by J. H. Randall, Jr., in *The Making of the Modern Mind* (rev ed.; Boston, 1940), p. 401.
5. Bertrand Russell, *The Problems of Philosophy* (London, 1948), p. 94.
6. See *infra*, pp. 56-60.
7. A few abstract terms toward which Hamann adopted a positive attitude in connection with his own use of them are: *Erfahrung, Evidenz, Geschichte, Glaube, Offenbarung, Natur, Vorsehung, Wahrheit.*
8. Josef Nadler terms Hamann's philosophy nominalistic, *Hamann, Kant, Goethe*, p. 42.
9. See Russell, *op. cit.*, p. 95.
10. *Ibid.*
11. Metzke, *op. cit.*, p. 54.
12. Ida Axelrod, "Johann Georg Hamanns Weltanschauung in ihrer mystischen Entwicklung," *Euphorion* (1904), p. 437.
13. Hamann, VII, 10. Cf. VI, 49.
14. W. R. Inge, "Plotinus," *Encyclopaedia Britannica*, Vol. VIII (1941), 82.
15. Thus, whereas Metzke devotes several pages to Hamann's doctrine of time, he fails to do the same for space. To be sure, his whole thesis is designed to show that the Magus broke through the prevailing "thing-categories" of his time to categories of personal relationships. Metzke does not deal directly with the subject for the simple reason that Hamann does not.
16. Hamann, *Neue Hamanniana*, p. 116.
17. Metzke, *op. cit.*, p. 55.
18. Metzke, *op. cit.*, pp. 54-57.
19. Moses Mendelssohn, *Jerusalem, Schriften*, ed. Moritz Brasch (Leipzig, 1880), Part II, p. 419.
20. Erwin Metzke, who was kind enough to read the present study in manuscript form, has written me as follows: "Ich finde Ihr Ausgehen von der Frage einer Ueberwindung des Subjekt-Objekt-Schemas sehr fruchtbar. Auch die Art wie Sie das Sprachproblem in den Mittelpunkt rücken, scheint mir sehr geeignet zu sein, um Hamann positiv zu beleuchten." (Letter, August 9, 1951).
21. Blanke, *Gottessprache und Menschensprache bei J. G. Hamann*, col. 205.
22. Unger, *Hamann und die Aufklärung*, I, 274.
23. Emil Brunner, *God and Man* (London, 1936), p. 48.
24. Hamann, G, V, 49. The only difference Hamann saw between Spinoza and Kant in this regard is revealed in the declaration that "Spinoza redet von einem Objekt *causa sui* und Kant von einem Subjekt *causa sui*." G, V, 406.
25. See Russell, *op. cit.*, p. 95. For a discussion of the metaphysical monist's inability to cope with the problem of relations, see Russell, *Philosophy* (New York, 1927), pp. 250 ff.
26. René Descartes, *The Method, Meditations and Philosophy of Descartes*, trans. and ed. John Veitch (New York, [n.d.] ), p. 171.
27. Hamann, G, V, 81, 476-477.
28. As in the case of F. H. Bradley. See *Appearance and Reality* (London, 1920), *passim*.
29. See Fritz Thoms, *Hamanns Bekehrung* (Gütersloh, 1933), pp. 103-129.
30. *Ibid.*, p. 129.
31. Unger, *Sprachtheorie*, p. 85.
32. See Ernst Cassirer, "Rationalism," *Encyclopaedia Britannica*, Vol. XVIII (1941), 992.
33. According to Kant, the "conception of the noumenon" is "connected with the limitation of sensibility." *Critique of Pure Reason*, trans. J. M. D. Meiklejohn (London, 1855), p. 187. Of this Kantian doctrine Hamann complained: "Leider gibt es keine Objekte mehr, sondern lauter Phänomene von ihnen." G, V, 313.

34. H.'s italics. G, V, 506; cf. 492-493. Cf. Merlan, "From Hume to Hamann."
35. Cf. John, 6:9 ff.
36. Jespersen, *The Philosophy of Grammar*, p. 33. Linguistic symbols of this type vary from language to language, but are always present in one form or another. For a systematic classification of them, see Hermann Paul, *Principles of the History of Language*, trans. H. A. Strong (new and rev. ed.; London, 1891), pp. 111-112. Relations between words sometimes act as symbols. The fact that word-relations may be utilized to represent non-verbal relations may not be construed to mean that such a linguistic device is any less symbolic than either a word which stands for a relation or for a concrete entity. It is the inevitable symbolic nature of all linguistic signs which Hamann's theory requires. For a discussion of this problem, see Bertrand Russell, *Philosophy*, pp. 264 ff., and Ludwig Wittgenstein, *Tractatus Logico-Politicus* trans. C. K. Ogden (London, 1922).
37. For prepositions as indicating relations, see Russell, *The Problems of Philosophy*, pp. 319-141, 149. It is assumed that all other "empty words" or syntactical devices of natural language refer to relations of space or time. I have confined myself to such symbols in the interest of simplicity and clarity. Other classes of words such as verbs might be used as examples of relational symbolism.
38. One writer illustrates the confusion that results, when the connective words characteristic of English are omitted from a given statement. He strikes the connective words out of the first sentence of the Declaration of Independence and compares his version with the original. The difference between the two versions is illuminating, but he still retains the characteristic English word-order, which is in itself one of the most important connective devices in that language. It would be necessary to eliminate entirely the characteristic sequence of words in English to note clearly the chaos which results from abstracting all connective devices. James C. Fernald, *Connectives of English Speech* (New York, 1904), pp. vii-viii.
39. Unger, *Sprachtheorie*, pp. 143-144.
40. *Ibid.*, pp. 67, 71 f., 80, 143, 144.
41. *Ibid.*, p. 150.
42. Sapir discusses the transformation of relational words into other parts of speech in *Language: An Introduction to the Study of Speech* (New York, 1921), p. 125.
43. There is one reference connecting the philosophic "custom of transforming every idea as well as bodily object into a person" with a distinction between parts of speech, but his meaning is quite obscure. Hamann, G, V, 683.
44. Although the approach and emphases of modern language philosophers vary, they all concur in their judgment as to the relevance of meaning. At least this much thinkers like Erdmann, Ogden, Richards, Carnap, Morris, Russell, Whitehead, Cassirer, and Urban have in common.
45. By "semantics" Jespersen meant simply the problem of meaning, and had no reference to a positivistic school of linguistic philosophy. The term "semantics" denoting the science of word meaning derives from Michel Bréal (1832-1912). See his *Essai de Sémantique: Science des Significations* (3rd.; Paris, 1904), p. 8.
46. Jespersen, *The Philosophy of Grammar*, p. 35.
47. Hamann, II, 210. The Magus' keen insight into the evolution of historical vernaculars is well attested by his recognition that the Greek dialect of Palestine, and particularly Galilee, represented an environmentally-conditioned variation of Attic Greek. In this connection, he compared the fate of the French language in London and Berlin to the fate of the Greek language in Palestine. Written at a time when the controversy over the relation of the Septuagint and New Testament Greek to the classical language was still far from settlement (1759),

this opinion provides an interesting incunabulum in the history of Biblical criticism.
48. See Joseph Nadler, *Die Hamannausgabe*, pp. 91 ff. Hamann is also an important source of the romantic idea of the unity of the arts. Josef Müller-Blattau says in this connection: "Der Kerngedanke Hamanns von der Urverbundenheit von Wort und Ton hatte sich im Volkslied musikalisch ausgewirkt, der Kerngedanke von der Zusammengehörigkeit der Künste, von Sprache, Musik und Gebärde hatte zur Schaffung der Idee des Musikdramas als eines Gesamtkunstwerkes geführt." *Hamann und Herder in ihren Beziehungen zur Musik* (Königsberg, 1931), pp. 26-27. The great importance of Hamann's theory of language for musical practice and theory in general is also stressed: "Die eigentliche und tiefste Einwirkung Hamanns und Herders in die Zeit hinein liegt in der Prägung bestimmter grosser Leitgedanken der Erneuerung von Musikübung und Musikauffassung. *Ihre Wurzeln sind Hamanns Gedanken über Sprache und Wort.*" (my italics) *Ibid.*, p. 19. See also Alfred R. Neumann, "The Evolution of the Concept Gesamtkunstwerk in German Romanticism." (Unpublished Ph.D. dissertation, Department of German, University of Michigan, 1951), p. 97.
49. Johann Wolfgang von Goethe, *Goethes Gespräche*, ed. F. W. von Biedermann (2d ed.; Leipzig, 1909), I, 43.
50. See Johann Wolfgang von Goethe, *Goethes Gespräche mit Eckermann*, ed. F. Deibel (Leipzig, 1908), II, 94.
51. The importance of Hamann's doctrine of creation is stressed by Fritz Blanke in his *J. G. Hamann als Theologe* (Tübingen, 1928), pp. 8 ff.
52. For interesting discussions of Herder's theory, see Steinthal, *op. cit.*, pp. 27-41; Jespersen, *Language*, pp. 26-29.
53. For Hamann's theory, see Steinthal, *op. cit.*, pp. 42-59; Unger, *Sprachtheorie* pp. 155-187; Blanke, *Gottessprache und Menschensprache bei J. G. Hamann*, cols. 206-207; Josef Nadler, *Johann Georg Hamann: der Zeuge des Corpus Mysticum*, pp. 199 ff.
54. According to Jespersen, *Language*, p. 28, Herder conceived of mind as an "unanalysable" entity.
55. Delff, *op. cit.*, p. 463.

## NOTES TO CHAPTER IV

1. (Unpublished item from Roth's *Nachlass*). Quoted by Metzke, *op. cit.*, p. 42.
2. "Johann Georg Hamann," *Encyclopaedia Britannica*, Vol. XI (1941), p. 115. Hamann is not the only philosopher opposed to abstract terminology. Students of American philosophy will be interested in Emerson's parallel opinion of the Hegelian nomenclature. See Henry A. Pochmann, *New England Transcendentalism and St. Louis Hegelianism* (Philadelphia, 1948), pp. 55 ff.
3. See Hamann, III, 253; IV, 301; VI, 35.
4. See Hamann, VII, 35, 125; G, V, 513.
5. Hamann was undoubtedly influenced by the general hostility to Spinoza prevalent in the eighteenth century. For a description of the prevailing attitude, see Bertrand Russell, *A History of Western Philosophy* (New York, 1945), p. 569. Oddly enough, however, one writer has charged Hamann with Spinozism, Steinthal, *op. cit.*, p. 59.
6. Windelband, *op. cit.*, p. 510.
7. Martin Luther, *Werke* (complete ed.; Weimar, Böhlau, 1883), I, 226.
8. "Hamann und Lessing," *Zeitschrift für systematische Theologie*, p. 188. Josef Nadler calls Hamann in one of his most recent works "einer der gerechtesten Beurteiler Lessings." *Geschichte der deutschen Literatur* (Vienna, 1951), p. 217.
9. See Blanke, "Hamann und Lessing," pp. 190 ff.

## NOTES TO CHAPTER IV

10. See G. E. Lessing, *Sämtliche Schriften*, eds. Karl Lachmann and Franz Muncker (Leipzig, 1897), XIII, 416.
11. Hamann, VI, 128. But Hamann was not without appreciation for Lessing's pioneering spirit. See VII, 239.
12. Consider the attitude of the two men toward Gottsched as expressed in Lessing's seventeenth *Literaturbrief* and in Hamann's *Versuch über eine akademische Frage*, II, 124.
13. Hamann's most important encounter with Wolffiannism was the variety represented by J. D. Michaelis and Moses Mendelssohn. The latter's inclination to equate the special revelation of the Old Testament with natural religion was anathema to Hamann. See VII, 17-70.
14. For Hamann's relation to Luther, see Fritz Blanke, "Hamann und Luther," *Luther-Jahrbuch*, X (1923), 28-55.
15. According to Matthijs Jolles, the basic idea of Lessing's fragmentary youthful poem, "Die Religion," is that religion in itself is neither good nor evil; the use to which it is put is decisive. Like fire it may be destructive or constructive. Presumably reason or "clear thinking" is the criterion by which religion is judged and guided. Here, as in the *Education of the Human Race*, reason is the last court of appeal. "Das religiöse Jugendbekenntnis Lessings," *Deutsche Beiträge* (Chicago, 1947), p. 117.
16. Thus Leibniz: "Always in every true affirmative proposition, whether necessary or contingent, universal or singular, the notion of the predicate is in some way comprehended in that of the subject, *praedictum inest subjecto;* otherwise, I know not what truth is." *Lettre au Prince Ernst* (1686). For the connection of this principle with "sufficient reason," see Leibniz, *op. cit.*, pp. 60 ff. For Hamann's attitude toward the latter, see III, 85, 86; VI, 284; G, V, 49.
17. See Lessing, *op. cit.*, p. 433.
18. Cf. the statement of Matthijs Jolles on the same subject. "Lessing's Conception of History," *Modern Philology*, XLIII, No. 3 (February, 1946), 188.
19. Emil Brunner, *Man in Revolt*, trans. Olive Wyon (New York), p. 101.
20. Lessing, *op. cit.*, p. 5.
21. *Ibid.*
22. Blanke, "Hamann und Lessing," *Zeitschrift für systematische Theologie*, p. 191.
23. Heinrich Weber has devoted a long treatise to the relationship of these two men. Though excellent for the details of their personal relationship, it fails to deal adequately with their theoretical differences. See Heinrich Weber, *op. cit.* See also the review of this work, Wilhelm Lütgert, "Hamann und Kant," *Kantstudien*, XI (1906), 118-125. Other excellent studies of the relationship of Hamann and Kant are to be found in Metzke, *op. cit.*, pp. 43-47, 142-144, and in Nadler, *Johann Georg Hamann: der Zeuge des Corpus Mysticum*, pp. 95-100, 224-225, 315-318, 348-354.
24. Heinrich Weber, *Hamann und Kant*, pp. 23 ff. This venture certainly constitutes a curious episode in the life of Kant. See also Hamann, I, 408,409.
25. See Heinrich Weber, *op. cit.*, pp. 35 ff.; Hamann, II, 443 ff.
26. See Karl Rosenkranz, *Geschichte der Kantschen Philosophie* (Leipzig, 1840), pp. 109-110.
27. Unger, *Sprachtheorie*, p. 230. Cf. Heinrich Weber, *op. cit.*, p. 226. Only on the basis of this low estimate of Hamann's critique of Kant could it be possible for an eminent scholar to write over one thousand pages on Kant's philosophy without once mentioning Hamann! See Edward Caird, *The Critical Philosophy of Immanuel Kant.* (Glasgow, 1909), 2 Vols.
28. See Blanke, *J. G. Hamann als Theologe*, pp. 13-14.

29. See Josef Nadler, *Hamann, Kant, Goethe*, pp. 42-43.
30. Metzke characterizes the *Metakritik* as "the most concentrated attack against Kant which has ever been written." Metzke, *op. cit.*, p. 44.
31. Metzke's work, already cited, received this award.
32. Goethe, *The Autobiography of Goethe*, I, 447.
33. Russell, *The Scientific Outlook*, op. cit., p. 82.
34. See Gervinus, *op. cit.*, p. 488
35. Unger, *Sprachtheorie*, p. 150.
36. Alfred North Whitehead, *Science and the Modern World* (New York, 1931), p. 26.
37. Kant, *op. cit.*, p. xx.
38. For a discussion of the generally slow reaction to Kant's *Critique*, see M. Kronenberg, *Kant: sein Leben und seine Lehre* (6th ed.; Munich, 1922), pp. 55 ff.
39. Mendelssohn, *op. cit.*, Part I, p. 299.
40. *Ibid.*, p. 300.
41. Harald Höffding, *A History of Modern Philosophy*, trans. B. E. Meyer (London, 1935), II, 11.
42. Metzke, *op. cit.*, p. 43.
43. Kant, *op. cit.*, p. xx
44. See Heinrich Weber, *op. cit.*, p. 201. See also Hamann, VII, 6.
45. Hamann, VII, 8. Blanke concurs in Hamann's opinion of Kant regarding this point. See *J. G. Hamann als Theologe*, pp. 13-14. Likewise Cassirer, "Goethe and the Kantian Philosophy," *Rousseau, Kant, Goethe*, trans. James Gutmann et al. (Princeton, 1947), p. 62.
46. Consider the statement of Cassirer in his comparison of Goethe and Kant: "Goethe does not think like Kant in terms of mere relations; he can only think in intuitive forms." "Goethe and Kantian Philosophy," *Rousseau, Kant, Goethe*, p. 92.
47. Kant, *op. cit.*, p. 35.
48. Hamann, G, V, 513. Cf. 109; VII, 216.
49. See Hamann, VI, 49-50; VII, 7-10; G, V, 16, 21-22, 505, 513, 515, 686, *et passim*.
50. Blanke, *Hamann als Theologe*, p. 6.
51. See Unger, *Sprachtheorie*, p. 214.
52. Hegel, *op. cit.*, p. 83.
53. For a treatment of what Metzke calls "das Geheimnisvolle der Wirklichkeit" in Hamann's thought, see Metzke, *op. cit.*, pp. 47 ff.
54. See Norman Kemp Smith, *A Commentary to Kant's Critique of Pure Reason* (London, 1918), p. 77.
55. Hamann, G, V, 494. Cf. 195, 199.
56. Cf. the opinion of Fritz Mauthner, *op. cit.*, p. xv.
57. It is illuminating to compare Hamann's appeal to ordinary language for a demonstration of the irreducibles of cognition to a similar effort by the contemporary language philosopher, Richard Albert Wilson, *op. cit.*, pp. 220 ff. Like Hamann, this thinker considers the problem of language meaningless apart from theological presuppositions. To be sure, his emergent evolutionism is quite distinct from Hamann's supernaturalism, but both are essentially theological principles.
58. Karl Barth speaks of the fertilizing effect of the "irreguläre Dogmatiker" like Hamann upon Christian theology. *Kirchliche Dogmatik* (Munich, 1932), I, Part I, 294.
59. See Étienne Gilson, *Reason and Revelation in the Middle Ages* (New York, 1938), pp. 8 ff. Tertullian's attitude toward the classical culture of Greece and Rome is not shared by Hamann. For in Hamann's view Athens has indeed a great deal to do with Jerusalem, and the Academy with the church. See Hamann, II, 42. Although it is possible to cite passages by Hamann decrying the excessive worship of classical antiquity,

on the whole he adopted a positive attitude toward it. See Josef Nadler, *Johann Georg Hamann: der Zeuge des Corpus Mysticum*, p. 21.
60. Gilson, *op. cit.*, pp. 38 ff.
61. Hamann was no Barthian. For him there is no discontinuity between nature and grace. See especially, Hamann, I, 54-55.
62. Russell, *A History of Western Philosophy*, p. 595.

## NOTES TO CHAPTER V

1. As a believing Lutheran, Hamann was a trinitarian. His writings are replete with evidence that God was real for him as Father, Son, and Holy spirit. This poses, to be sure, the classic Christian problem of accepting at once the unity of the Godhead and its diversity as a Triune Person. Hamann tended to find the uniting element of the Godhead in the divine humility (*Demut*) especially in the *Kleeblatt hellenistischer Briefe*, but did not dwell upon this. See Hamann, II, 207. Nadler in his excellent, though perhaps too mystical, interpretation of Hamann emphasizes the latter's trinitarianism and the influence of Philo and the church fathers on his philosophy of religion. See *Johann Georg Hamann: der Zeuge des Corpus Mysticum*, 21 ff. et passim.
2. Hamann, VII, 151-152. Cf. VI, 365, 370 ff.; G, V, 406.

## SELECTED BIBLIOGRAPHY

(Only those works cited or referred to in text or notes are included)

Axelrod, Ida G. "Johann Georg Hamanns Weltanschauung in ihrer mystischen Entwicklung," *Euphorion*, XI (1904), 433-457.
Barth, Karl. *Kirchliche Dogmatik*. Vol. I. Munich: Christian Kaiser Verlag, 1932.
Bauke, Hermann. *Die Probleme der Theologie Calvins*. Leipzig: J. C. Hinrich'sche Buchhandlung, 1928.
Belgion, Montgomery. "Review of Walter Lowrie, *Johann Georg Hamann: An Existentialist*," *Theology*, LIV, No. 376 (October, 1951), 389-391.
Benz, Richard E. *Sprach-und Volkserlebnis bei Hamann und Herder*. Sonderdruck aus der wissenschaftlichen Festschrift zur 700 Jahr-Feier der Kreuzschule zu Dresden, 1926.
Blanke, Fritz. "Gottessprache und Menschensprache bei J. G. Hamann," *Theologische Blätter*, IX, No. 8 (August, 1930), cols. 201-210.
―――. "Hamann und Lessing," *Zeitschrift für systematische Theologie*, VI, No. 1 (1929), 188-210.
―――. "Hamann und Luther," *Luther-Jahrbuch*, X (1928), 28-55.
―――. *J. G. Hamann als Theologe*. Tübingen: Verlag von J. C. B. Mohr, 1928.
Bradley, F. H. *Appearance and Reality*. London: George Allen and Unwin, Ltd., 1920.
Bréal, Michel. *Essai de Sémantique: Science des Significations*. 3rd ed. revised. Paris: Libraire Hachette et Cie., 1904.
Brown, Francis Andrew. "Hamann's Opinion of Muralt," *Journal of English and Germanic Philology*, XLVII, No. 1 (January, 1948), 53-58.
Brunner, Emil. *God and Man*. London: Student Christian Movement Press, 1936.
―――. *Man in Revolt*. Translated by Olive Wyon. New York: Charles Scribner's Sons, 1939.
Buckham, John Wright. "Mysticism," *Encyclopedia of Religion*. Edited by Vergilius Ferm. New York: Philosophical Library, 1945, pp. 513-514.
Burger, Ewald. *J. G. Hamann: Schöpfung und Erlösung im Irrationalismus* Göttingen: Vandenhoeck & Ruprecht, 1929.
Burschell, Friedrich. "Ueber Johann Georg Hamann," *Logos*, IV (1913), 100-109.
Caird, Edward. *The Critical Philosophy of Immanuel Kant*. 2d ed. Glasgow: James Maclehose, 1909.
Cassirer, Ernst. *Die Philosophie der symbolischen Formen*. Vol. I. Berlin: Bruno Cassirer Verlag, 1923.
―――. *Idee und Gestalt*. Berlin: Bruno Cassirer Verlag, 1921.
―――. "Rationalism," *Encyclopaedia Britannica*. Vol. XVIII (1941), 991-993.
―――. "Goethe and the Kantian Philosophy," *Rousseau, Kant, Goethe*. Translated by James Gutmann et al. Princeton: Princeton University Press, 1947. Pp. 61-98.
Clark, Robert T. "Hamann's Opinion of Herder's *Ursachen des gesunkenen Geschmacks*," *Modern Language Notes*, LXI, No. 2 (February, 1946), 94-99.
Delff, Hugo. "Johann Georg Hamann," *Allgemeine Deutsche Biographie*. Vol. X (1879), 456-468.
Descartes, René. *The Method, Meditations and Philosophy of Descartes*. Translated by John Veitch. New York: Tudor Publishing Co. [n.d.]
Dyrssen, Carl. "Hamann und Oetinger," *Zeitwende*, I (1925), 376-396.
Ernst, Paul. *Hamann und Bengel*. Königsberg: Gräfe und Unzer Verlag, 1935.

Ewing, A. C. "Kantianism," *Twentieth Century Philosophy*. Edited by Dagobert D. Runes. New York: Philosophical Library, 1943. Pp. 251-263.
Fernald, James C. *Connectives of English Speech*. New York: Funk and Wagnalls, 1904.
Gervinus, G. G. *Geschichte der deutschen Dichtung*. Edited by Karl Bartsch. Vol. IV. 5th ed. Leipzig: Verlag von Wilhelm Engelmann, 1873.
Gilson, Étienne. *Reason and Revelation in the Middle Ages*. New York: Charles Scribner's Sons, 1938.
Goethe, Johann Wolfgang von. *The Autobiography of Goethe*. Translated by John Oxenford. Vol. I. London: Henry G. Bohn, 1848.
———. *Goethe Gespräche*. Edited by Flodoard Woldemar von Biedermann. 2d ed. Leipzig: F. W. von Biedermann, 1909.
———. *Goethes Gespräche mit Eckermann*. Edited by Franz Deibel. Vol. II. 2d ed. Leipzig: Insel Verlag, 1908.
———. *Sämtliche Werke*. Jubiläumsausgabe. Vols. XXIV, XXVI. Stuttgart: J. G. Cotta'sche Buchhandlung Nachfolger [n.d.]
Grant, Frederick C. "Form Criticism," *Encyclopedia of Religion*. Edited by Vergilius Ferm. New York: Philosophical Library, 1945. P. 285.
Hamann, Johann Georg. *J. G. Hamanns, des Magus im Norden, Leben und Schriften*. Edited by C. H. Gildemeister. 6 vols. Gotha: Friedrich Andreas Perthes, 1857-73.
———. "The Merchant," *Prose Writers of Germany*. Anonymously translated. Edited by Frederic Hedge. 4th ed. New York: C. S. Francis and Co., 1856. Pp. 121-127.
———. *Neue Hamanniana*. Munich: C. H. Beck'sche Verlagsbuchhandlung, 1905.
———. *Sämtliche Werke*. Edited by Josef Nadler. Vols. II. Vienna: Verlag Herder. 1949-1950.
———. *Schriften*. Edited by Friedrich Roth and G. A. Wiener. 8 vols. Berlin: G. Reimer, 1821-43.
———. *Schriften J. G. Hamanns*. Edited by Karl Widmaier. Leipzig: Insel Verlag, 1921.
Heckel, Theodor. *Johann Georg Hamanns Briefe zur Einführung in Leben und Theologie*. Göttingen: Vandenhoeck and Ruprecht, 1944.
Hegel, G. W. F. *Werke*. Edited by Ph. Marheineke et al. Complete ed. Vol. XVII. Berlin: Verlag von Duncker und Humblot, 1885.
Herder, Johann Gottfried. *Sämtliche Werke*. Edited by Bernhard Suphan. Vol. V. Berlin: Weidmannsche Buchhandlung, 1891.
Hettner, Hermann. *Geschichte der deutschen Literatur im achtzehnten Jahrhundert*. Edited by Georg Witkowski. Leipzig: Paul List Verlag, 1928.
Hilpert, Walter. *Johann Georg Hamann als Kritiker der deutschen Literatur*. Königsberg: Schulz, 1931.
Höffding, Harald. *A History of Modern Philosophy*. Translated by B. E. Meyer. Vol. II. London: Macmillan, 1935.
Imendörfer, Nora. *Johann Georg Hamann und seine Bücherei*. Königsberg: Ost-Europa Verlag, 1938.
Inge, W. R. "Plotinus," *Encyclopaedia Britannica*, Vol. XVIII (1941), 81-83.
Ipsen, Gunther. *Sprachphilosophie der Gegenwart*. Berlin: Junker und Dünnhaupt Verlag, 1930.
Jespersen, Otto. *The Philosophy of Grammar*. London: George Allen and Unwin, Ltd., 1925.
———. *Language: Its Nature, Development, and Origin*. New York: Henry Holt and Co., 1925.
"Johann Georg Hamann," *Encyclopaedia Britannica*. Vol. XI (1941), 115.
Jolles, Matthijs. "Das religiöse Jugendbekenntnis Lessings," *Deutsche Beiträge zur geistigen Ueberlieferung*. Edited by Arnold Bergstraesser et al. Chicago: University of Chicago Press, 1947. Pp. 115-133.

———. "Lessing's Conception of History," *Modern Philology*, XLIII, No. 3 (February, 1946), 175-191.
Kant, Immanuel. *Critique of Pure Reason.* Translated by J. M. D. Meiklejohn. London: Henry G. Bohn, 1855.
Kierkegaard, Søren. *Concluding Unscientific Postscript.* Translated by David F. Swenson and Walter Lowrie. Princeton: Princeton University Press, 1944.
Kind, John L. *Edward Young in Germany.* New York: The Columbia University Press, 1906.
Klossowski, Pierre. *Les Méditations Bibliques de Hamann.* Paris: Les Éditions de Minuit, 1948.
Korff, H. A. *Der Geist der Goethezeit.* Vol. I. Leipzig: Verlagsbuchhandlung von J. J. Weber, 1923.
Kowalewski, Arnold. "Hamann als religiöser Lebensphilosoph," *Bilder aus dem religiösen und kirchlichen Leben Ostpreussens.* Königsberg: Gräfe und Unzer, 1927.
Kraemer, H. *The Christian Message in a Non-Christian World.* London: Edinburg House Press, 1938.
Kronenberg, M. *Kant: sein Leben und sein Werk.* 6th ed. Revised. Munich: C. H. Beck'sche Verlagsbuchhandlung, 1922.
Küsters, Marie Theres. *Inhaltsanalyse von J. Georg Hamanns Aesthetica in Nuce.* Bottrop, Westphalia: Postberg Verlag, 1936.
Leese, Kurt. *Krisis und Wende des christlichen Geistes.* 2d ed. revised. Berlin: Junker und Dünnhaupt, Verlag, 1941.
Leibniz, Gottfried Wilhelm. *The Monadology.* Edited and translated by Robert Latta. London: Oxford University Press, 1948.
Lessing, G. E. *Sämtliche Schriften.* Edited by Karl Lachmann and Franz Muncker. Vol. XIII Leipzig: Göschen, 1897.
Lowrie, Walter. *Johann Georg Hamann: An Existentialist.* Princeton: Princeton Theological Seminary, 1950.
———, *Kierkegaard.* London: Oxford University Press, 1938.
Lütgert, Wilhelm. "Hamann und Kant," *Kantstudien*, XI (1936), 118-125.
———, *Die Religion des deutschen Idealismus und ihr Ende.* Gütersloh: Bertelsmann, 1923.
Luther, Martin. *Kritische Gesamtausgabe.* Vol. I. Weimar: Hermann Böhlau, 1883.
Mauthner, Fritz. *Beiträge zu einer Kritik der Sprache.* 3d ed. Vol. I. Stuttgart: Cotta, 1912.
Mendelssohn, Moses. *Schriften.* Edited by Mortiz Brasch. Leipzig: Verlag von Leopold Voss, 1880.
Merlan, Philip. "From Hume to Hamann," *The Personalist*, XXXII, No. 1 (Winter, January, 1951), 11-18.
———, "J. G. Hamann as Spokesman of the Middle Class," *Journal of the History of Ideas*, IX, No. 3 (June, 1948), 380-384.
Metzke, Erwin. *J. G. Hamanns Stellung in der Philosophie des 18. Jahrhunderts.* Halle/Saale: Max Niemeyer Verlag, 1934.
Minor, Jakob. *Johann Georg Hamann in seiner Bedeutung für die Sturm- und Drangperiode.* Frankfurt am Main: Rütten & Loening, 1881.
Müller-Blattau, Josef. *Hamann und Herder in ihren Beziehungen zur Musik.* Königsberg: Gräfe und Unzer Verlag, 1931.
Nadler, Josef. *Die Geschichte der deutschen Literatur.* Vienna: Johannes Günther Verlag, 1951.
———, *Die Hamannausgabe.* Halle/Saale: Max Niemeyer Verlag, 1930.
———, *Hamann, Kant, Goethe.* Halle/Saale: Max Niemeyer Verlag, 1931.
———, *Johann Georg Hamann: der Zeuge des Corpus Mysticum.* Salzburg: Otto Müller Verlag, 1949.
Nadler, Käte. "Hamann und Hegel: Zum Verhältnis von Dialektik und Existentialität," *Logos*, XX (1931), 259-285.
Neumann, Alfred R. "The Evolution of the Concept Gesamtkunstwerk in

German Romanticism." Unpublished Ph.D. dissertation, Department of German, University of Michigan, 1951.
O'Flaherty, James C. "J. D. Michaelis: Rational Biblicist," *Journal of English and Germanic Philology*, XLIX, No. 2 (April, 1950), 172-181.
Paul, Hermann. *Principles of the History of Language*. Translated by H. A. Strong. New and rev. ed. London: Longmans, Green, and Co., 1891.
Peirce, C. S. *The Philosophy of Peirce*. Edited by Justus Buchler. New York: Harcourt, Brace & Co., 1940.
Peterson, Erik. "Das Problem der Bibelauslegung im Pietismus des 18. Jahrhunderts," *Zeitschrift für systematische Theologie*, I (1923), 468-481.
Pochmann, Henry A. *New England Transcendentalism and St. Louis Hegelianism*. Philadelphia: Carl Schurz Memorial Foundation, 1948.
*Publications of the Modern Language Association*, LXVI, No. 3 (April, 1951).
Randall, John Herman, Jr. *The Making of the Modern Mind*. Revised ed. New York: Houghton Mifflin Co., 1940.
Raumer, Karl von, "Johann Georg Hamann," *American Journal of Education*, XI (1859), 247-259.
Richter, Helene. "Blake und Hamann," *Archiv für das Studium der neueren Sprachen und Literatures*, CLVIII (1930), 213-221, CLIX 1931), 36-45, 195-210.
Rodemann, Wilhelm. *Hamann und Kierkegaard*. Gütersloh: Bertelsmann, 1922.
Rosenkranz, Karl. *Geschichte der Kantschen Philosophie*. Leipzig: Verlag von Leopold Voss, 1840.
Russell, Bertrand. *A History of Western Philosophy*. New York: Simon and Schuster, 1945.
———. *Philosophy*. New York: Norton, 1927.
———. *The Problems of Philosophy*. London: Oxford University Press, 1948.
———. *The Scientific Outlook*. New York: Norton, 1931.
Säemann, Edith. *J. G. Hamann und die französiche Literatur*. Königsberg: Schulz, 1931.
Sapir, Edward. *Language: An Introduction to the Study of Speech*. New York: Harcourt, Brace and Company, 1921.
Schack, Tage. *Johann Georg Hamann*. Copenhagen: Tidehvervs Forlag, 1948.
Schlichtegroll, Friedrich. *Biographie des königlichen preussischen Geheimenkriegsrats zu Königsberg, Theodor Gottlieb von Hippel, zum Teil von ihm selbst verfasst*. Gotha: Friedrich Andreas Perthes, 1801.
Schoonhoven, E. Jansen. *Natuur en Genade bij J. G. Hamann*. Nijkerk: G. F. Callenbach, 1945.
Schmitz, F. J. *The Problem of Individualism and the Crises in the Lives of Lessing and Hamann*. Los Angeles: University of California Press, 1944.
Schreiner, Helmuth. *Die Menschwerdung Gottes in der Theologie Johann Georg Hamanns*. Stuttgart: Furche Verlag, 1946.
Smith, Norman Kemp. *A Commentary to Kant's 'Critique of Pure Reason.'* London: Macmillan Co., 1918.
Smith, Ronald Gregor. "The Living and Speaking God," *Hibbert Journal*, XLII, No. 3 (April, 1944), 198-203.
Stalin, Joseph. "On Several Problems of Linguistics," *The Soviet Linguistic Controversy*. Translated by John V. Murra et al., pp. 86-87.
Steinthal, H. *Der Ursprung der Sprache*. Berlin: Ferd. Dümmlers Buchhandlung, 1851.
Stephan, Horst. "Ein Ahnherr des modernen Christentums," *Die Christliche Welt*, XVI, No. 36 (September 4, 1902), col. 854.
Thoms, Fritz. *Hamanns Bekehrung*. Gütersloh: "Der Rufer" Evangelischer Verlag, 1933.

Thornton, Agathe H. F. "The Hebrew Conception of Speech as Creative Energy," *Hibbert Journal* XLIV, No. 2 (January, 1946), 132-134.
Unger, Rudolf. *Johann Georg Hamann: Sibyllinische Blätter des Magus.* Jena and Leipzig: 1905.
———, *Hamanns Sprachtheorie im Zusammenhang seines Denkens.* Munich: C. H. Beck'sche Verlagsbuchhandlung, 1905.
———, *Hamann und die Aufklärung.* 2 vols. Jena: Eugen Diederichs, 1911.
———. "Hamann und die Empfindsamkeit," *Euphorion,* XXX (1929), 169-170.
———. "Johann Georg Hamann," *Die Grossen Deutschen: neue Deutsche Biographie.* Edited by Willy Andreas and Wilhelm von Scholz. Vol. II. Berlin: Propyläen Verlag, 1935, 277-289.
Urban, Wilbur Marshall. *Language and Reality.* London: George Allen and Unwin, Ltd., 1939.
Vossler, Karl. *The Spirit of Language in Civilization.* Translated by Oscar Oeser. New York: Harcourt, Brace and Co., 1932.
Wahl, Jean. *Études Kierkegaardiennes.* 2d. ed. Paris: Librairie Philosophique J. Vrin, 1949.
Watson, John B. *Behaviorism.* New York: Norton, 1925.
Weber, Hans Emil. "Zwei Propheten des Irrationalismus," *Neue kirchliche Zeitschrift,* XXVIII (1917), 23-58.
Weber, Heinrich. *Hamann und Kant.* Munich: C. H. Beck'sche Verlagsbuchhandlung, 1904.
Whitehead, Alfred North. *Process and Reality.* New York: Macmillan, 1930.
———. *Science and the Modern World.* New York: Macmillan, 1931.
———. *Symbolism: Its Meaning and Effect.* New York: MacMillan, 1927.
Wilson, Richard Albert. *The Miraculous Birth of Language.* New York: Philosophical Library, 1948.
Windelband, W. *A History of Philosophy.* Translated by James H. Tufts. 2d ed. New York: Macmillan, 1914.
Wittgenstein, Ludwig. *Tractatus Logico-Politicus.* Translated by C. K. Ogden. London: Kegan Paul, Trench, Trubner, 1922.

# INDEX OF PERSONS

## A

Aristotle, 77.
Arminius, 7.
Axelrod, Ida, 52, 108.

## B

Bach, Johann Sebastian, 106.
Bacon, Francis, 41, 60, 71.
Barth, Karl, 112.
Bauke, Hermann, 18, 104.
Belgion, Montgomery, 107.
Bengel, J. A., 105.
Benz, Richard E., 106.
Berens, J. C., 24, 81.
Bergson, Henri, 11, 29, 35.
Berkeley, George, 34, 54, 105.
Blake, William, 105.
Blanke, Fritz, 19, 56, 77, 81, 89, 101, 103, 104, 108, 110, 111, 112.
Boehme, Jakob, 41, 106.
Bradley, F. H., 5, 108.
Bréal, Michel, 109.
Brown, Francis Andrew, 107.
Brunner, Emil, 7, 57, 108, 111.
Bruno, Giordano, 33, 34, 58.
Buckham, John Wright, 106.
Burschell, Friedrich, 103, 104.

## C

Caird, Edward, 111.
Calvin, John, 18.
Carnap, Rudolf, 109.
Cassirer, Ernst, 5, 15, 35, 67, 101, 102, 103, 104, 106, 108, 109, 112.
Christ, 77, 78, 79, 80.
Clark, Robert T., 107.
Condillac, Étienne Bonnot de, 71.

## D

Darwin, Charles, 35.

Delff, Hugo, 73, 106, 107, 110.
Descartes, René, 35, 42, 58, 105, 108.
Dilthey, Wilhelm, 42.
Dyrssen, Carl, 101, 106.

## E

Erdmann, K. O., 109.
Ernst, Paul, 105.
Ewing, A. C., 105, 106.

## F

Fernald, James C., 109.
Funck, H., 102.

## G

Galileo, Galilei, 74.
Gallitzin, Princess Amalia, 59.
Gervinus, G. G., 102, 112.
Gildemeister, C. H., 101.
Gilson, Étienne, 112, 113.
Goethe, Johann Wolfgang von, 2, 6, 7, 11, 15, 70, 101, 102, 103, 104, 110, 112.
Gottsched, Johann Christoph, 111.
Grant, Frederick C., 103.
Green, Joseph, 24.

## H

Heckel, Theodor, 103.
Hegel, G. W. F., 10-11, 90, 102, 103, 112.
Hemsterhuis, Franz, 76.
Herder, Johann Gottfried, 6, 7, 10, 11, 23, 35, 36, 38, 59, 60, 70-72, 78, 84, 99, 110.
Hettner, Hermann, 6, 7, 102, 105.
Hilpert Walter, 107.
Hippel, Theodor Gottlieb, 104.
Hobbes, Thomas, 60.
Höffding, Harald, 83, 112.

Homer, 24, 45.
Humboldt, Karl Wilhelm von, 10, 35.
Hume, David, 11, 24, 41, 43, 54, 60, 61, 97.
Hutcheson, Francis, 107.

## I

Imendörffer, Nora, 104.
Inge, W. R., 108.
Ipsen, Gunther, 102.

## J

Jacobi, Friedrich Heinrich, 4, 11, 13, 25, 31, 48, 84, 90, 91, 101.
Jean Paul, 7.
Jespersen, Otto, 67, 101, 104, 105, 109, 110.
Jesus Christ (see Christ).
Jolles, Matthijs, 111.

## K

Kant, Immanuel, 6, 11, 13, 14, 22, 24, 35, 36, 39, 54, 56, 60, 61, 77, 81-91, 92, 94, 96, 97, 105, 106, 108, 111, 112.
Kepler, Johann, 74.
Kierkegaard, Søren, 7, 8, 102.
Kind, John L., 107.
Kleuker, Johann Friedrich, 102.
Klopstock, Gottlieb Friedrich, 22.
Klossowski, Pierre, 102.
Konschel, Paul, 102.
Korff, H. A., 40, 106.
Kowalewski, Arnold, 101.
Kraemer, H., 104.
Kronenberg, M., 112.
Küsters, Marie Theres, 102.

## L

Latta, Robert, 107.
Leese, Kurt, 102, 106.

Leibniz, Gottfried Wilhelm, 35, 42, 43, 55, 94, 106.
Lessing, Gotthold Ephraim, 42, 77-81, 84, 85, 90, 92, 94, 106, 110, 111.
Lindner, F. E., 26.
Lindner, J. G., 4.
Locke, John, 60, 71, 107.
Lowrie, Walter, 101, 102, 105.
Ludendorff, Erich, 7.
Lütgert, Wilhelm, 106, 111.
Luther, Martin, 18, 25, 77, 79, 107, 110.

## M

Mauthner, Fritz, 101, 112.
Melanchthon, Philipp, 18.
Merlan, Philip, 101, 109.
Mendelssohn, Moses, 11, 54, 83, 108, 111, 112.
Metzke, Erwin, 3, 11, 47, 52, 53, 81, 84, 101, 103, 105, 106, 107, 108, 110, 111, 112.
Michaelis, J. D., 13, 15, 103, 111.
Minor, Jakob, 6, 102, 107.
Morris, Charles W., 109.
Müller-Blattau, Josef, 110.

## N

Nadler, Josef, 7-8, 10, 24, 41, 81, 102, 103, 104, 106, 108, 110, 112, 113.
Nadler, Käte, 102.
Neumann, Alfred R., 110.
Newton, Isaac, 74.
Nicholas of Cusa, 33.

## O

Ogden, C. K., 109.

## P

Parmenides, 5.
Paul, Hermann, 109.
Paul, Jean (see Jean Paul).

## INDEX OF PERSONS

Peirce, C. S., 105.
Peterson, Erik, 101.
Philo Judaeus, 113.
Plato, 34, 43, 76, 105.
Plotinus, 34.
Pochmann, Henry A., 110.

### R

Raumer, Karl von, 103.
Reimarus, Hermann Samuel, 103.
Richards, I. A., 109.
Richter, Helene, 106.
Richter, Jean Paul Friedrich (see Jean Paul).
Rodemann, Wilhelm, 102.
Rosenkranz, Karl, 111.
Roth, Friedrich, 101.
Rousseau, Jean Jacques, 76.
Russell, Bertrand, 35, 51, 82, 94, 105, 106, 109, 110, 112, 113.

### S

Säemann, Edith, 107.
Saint Paul, 5.
Santayana, George, 47.
Sapir, Edward, 109.
Schack, Tage, 101, 107.
Schmitz, F. J., 106.
Schmitz-Kallenberg, Ludwig, 102.
Schoonhoven, E. Jansen, 107.
Schreiner, Helmuth, 106.
Shaftesbury, Anthony Ashley Cooper 3rd Earl of, 107.
Shakespeare, William, 23, 24, 45, 107.
Smith, Norman Kemp, 112.
Smith, Ronald Gregor, 104.
Socrates, 42, 43, 44, 53.
Spinoza, Baruch, 5, 42, 48, 53, 55, 57, 58, 76.
Stalin, Joseph, 1, 105.

Stephan, Horst, 107.
Steinthal, H., 101, 110.
Süssmilch, J. P., 71.
Swedenborg, Emanuel, 106.

### T

Tatman, T. C., 103.
Tertullian, 112.
Thoms, Fritz, 108.
Thornton, Agathe H. F., 104.
Troeltsch, Ernst, 42.

### U

Unger, Rudolf, 3, 4, 5, 10-11, 26, 29, 40, 47, 56, 63, 64, 65, 83, 98, 101, 102, 103, 104, 105, 107, 109, 110.
Urban, Wilbur Marshall, 32, 103, 105, 109.

### V

Vico, Giovanni Battista, 11.
Vossler, Karl, 101.

### W

Wahl, Jean, 102.
Watson, John B., 35, 106.
Weber, Heinrich, 102, 106, 111, 112.
Whitehead, Alfred North, 33, 35, 105, 109, 112.
Wiener, Gustaf A., 101.
Wilson, Richard Albert, 101.
Winckelmann, Johann Joachim, 42.
Windelband, W., 104, 110.
Wittgenstein, Ludwig, 109.
Wolff, Christian, 42, 60, 80, 84.

### Y

Young, Edward, 105, 107.

www.ingramcontent.com/pod-product-compliance
Lightning Source LLC
Chambersburg PA
CBHW031319150426
43191CB00005B/269